Edgar Cayce's Twelve Lessons in Personal Spirituality

D1566933

EDGAR CAYCE'S
TWELVE LESSONS
IN
PERSONAL SPIRITUALITY

by Kevin J. Todeschi

ASSOCIATION FOR
RESEARCH AND
ENLIGHTENMENT

A.R.E. Press • Virginia Beach • Virginia

A.R.E. Press
215 67th Street
Virginia Beach, VA 23451-2061

Library of Congress Cataloging-in-Publication Data
    Todeschi, Kevin J.
    Twelve lessons in personal spirituality : an overview of the
Edgar Cayce readings on personal transformation / by Kevin
J. Todeschi
        p. cm.
    ISBN 0-87604-369-4 (trade paper)
    1.Spiritual life. 2. Cayce, Edgar, 1877-1945. 3. Association
for Research and Enlightenment. I. Association for Research
and Enlightenment. II. Title. III. Series.
BP605.A77T63 1996
133.9-dc20   96-28324

Cover design by Richard Boyle

To Mary

*for helping me to understand what's at the core of
personal transformation*

Contents

Author's Note	*ix*
Preface	*xi*
The Twelve Lessons	*xv*
The Importance of Meditation in Personal *Transformation*	*xvii*

THE LESSONS:

Cooperation	1
Know Thyself	15
Ideals	30
Faith	44
Virtue and Understanding	56
Fellowship	68
Patience	82
The Open Door	96
In His Presence	110
The Cross and the Crown	124
Oneness	140
Love	154
Meditation Affirmations	*169*

Author's Note

The nature of our personal belief systems is appropriately described in the well-known story of the blind men and the elephant. Five blind men came upon an elephant in the jungle. One touched up against the creature's side, another took hold of its tail, the third felt its trunk, another grabbed an ear, and the fifth leaned against its leg. Each of the blind men took it upon themselves to describe the true nature of the elephant to the others. The first said, "The truth of the elephant is that he is very much like a wall." The second, who held the tail, said, "No, you are wrong, the elephant is like a rope." The third felt the skin of the creature's trunk and likened it to a snake. The fourth could not believe the erroneous perceptions of the other three and shook the elephant's ear as he spoke, "Are you all fools? The elephant is like a giant leaf!" And the fifth cried out for each of the others to listen to him as he pounded the elephant's leg for emphasis, "How can you be so wrong, for the truth of the elephant is he is much like a tree!?"

In varying degrees, each of us is like one of these five characters. Rather than standing back and becoming receptive to the possibility that there is much more to the elephant than we have currently come to grips with, we often become all the more focused on the reality of our individual perceptions. In an attempt to understand our truth, too often we put boundaries around what we believe in order to come to grips with it. Unfortunately, this approach blinds us to the insights and information that have become true for someone else—the very insights that might lead us even further along our own path and individual search for meaning.

Hopefully, a day will come in the not-too-distant future when each of us becomes a little more receptive to looking at the entire elephant.

Notes about the Edgar Cayce readings:

The Edgar Cayce readings are indexed by case number. For example, reading #262-3 refers to the third reading given in a series to case #262 (which was the original study group).

No attempt has been made to alter the language of the readings to be—what in common parlance is termed—"politically correct." Therefore, when using such terminology as "the nature of man," Cayce is not referring to gender; instead, the term would apply to all of humankind. In addition, the readings themselves appear to be rich with Christian terminology. However, Cayce often used terms and phrases that do not necessarily equate with their common usage. These differences are explained within the text. For example, "the Christ" can refer to Jesus, but it is also a pattern of consciousness which is the birthright of every soul—regardless of one's religious denomination.

Preface

In September 1931 a group of ordinary people met with Edgar Cayce, an individual whom many consider to be one of the greatest mystics of all time. Although the meeting had been called in order for each of them to work more personally with Cayce's psychic information, none of the group members could have possibly imagined the impact that meeting and their subsequent gatherings—nearly fifty meetings for the first twelve lessons—would have upon the rest of their lives, nor could the group have foreseen the effect of their work upon the lives of thousands of others even decades later.

Study Group #1, as they called themselves, worked for years to compile twelve essays in spirituality. Beginning with the lesson "Cooperation," the essays were assembled in book form and published in 1942 as *A Search for God, Book I.* The group's intent was to work with the material so it could be applied, understood, even "lived" in their daily lives. It was their hope that universal concepts might somehow be practically applied in such a manner as to bring a true awareness of the living Spirit into everyday life. In turn, they hoped that their relationships with those around them might somehow be positively affected through the process. The end result has been that these lessons in spirituality have been called one of the earliest and most effective tools for personal transformation introduced into the Western Hemisphere.

Although raised in a Christian upbringing, Cayce's information is deeply ecumenical. These lessons in spirituality emphasize the oneness of all life, a love and tolerance for all people, as well as a compassion and understanding for every major religion of the world. In fact, one of the most important steps to personal transformation deals with the importance of cultivating an awareness of our oneness with all other individuals. Coming to share that same understanding, Study Group #1's preface to *A Search for God, Book I,* ended with:

There is nothing new here. The search for God is as old as man. This book is passed on in the hope that through it, during the trying times ahead, many may glimpse a ray of light; that in other hearts it may awaken a new hope and vision of a better world through application of His laws in daily life.

Study Group #1 was told that they could "bring light to a waiting world" and that these lessons would still be studied a hundred years into the future. Today, many decades later, this material has been studied by thousands of individuals from every walk of life and religious background, enabling them to become more aware of themselves through cooperation, personal awareness, faith, meditation, and love. These interdenominational discussion groups examine this material on soul growth in individual homes all over the world. (If you are interested in visiting one of these groups, please contact A.R.E., 215 67th Street, Virginia Beach, VA 23451-2061.)

Since the Cayce work has been computerized, access

to particular information is readily available in ways that even Edgar Cayce might have hesitated to predict. In addition to utilizing the same resource material provided to the original study group, this volume presents a topical overview of the entire body of Edgar Cayce readings on each of the twelve lessons. Many of the readings discuss the same subjects which had been presented to Study Group #1, but it was not until 1971 that the material was sufficiently indexed so that any topic could be studied in a way not available to Cayce's early supporters. *Twelve Lessons in Personal Spirituality* is compiled in the hopes of serving one or more of the following purposes: as a tool for personal reflection and study, as a handbook for small group discussion, and even as a source of encouragement during those moments when the challenges of life seem more overwhelming than the beauty of it.

The hallmark of this material is that it suggests there is a definite purpose for living. There is also the promise that with a spiritual intent we can come to understand that purpose. We are all here for a reason, a reason that joins us in search of a common heritage. Though we may be separated by language, or religion, or customs, or race, or even vast distances, we all share the earth as our temporal home, we are all children of the same God, and we are all seekers along the way.

Kevin J. Todeschi
Virginia Beach, Virginia

THE TWELVE LESSONS

The purpose of the entity in the earth, is that it may know itself, also to be itself, and yet at one with the Creative Forces, fulfilling those purposes for which the entity comes into the earth; accepting, believing, knowing then thy relationship to that Creative Force. For He hath called thee friend; not servant, but a friend, a brother, a sister. 3508-1

The Importance of Meditation in Personal Transformation

For, ye must learn to meditate—just as ye have learned to walk, to talk . . .

Edgar Cayce reading 281-41

For countless individuals, the Edgar Cayce readings have been instrumental in providing them with an entirely new understanding of humankind's relationship to God. From Cayce's perspective, that relationship is not a thing far off—or something that is relegated to the "hereafter"—rather it is a personal connection that can be experienced right now in everyday life: *We are God's children, and He is mindful of us at all times!* Meditation is important because it can provide individuals with the means for gaining a personal awareness of that relationship:

What *is* Meditation? It is not musing, not daydreaming; but as ye find your bodies made up of the physical, mental and spiritual, it is the attuning of the mental body and the physical body to its spiritual source. Many say that ye have no consciousness of having a soul,—yet the very fact that ye hope, that ye have a desire for better things, the very fact that ye are able to be sorry or glad, indicates an activity of the mind that takes hold upon something that is not temporal in its nature—something that passeth not away with the last breath that is drawn but that takes hold upon the very sources of its beginning—the *soul*—that which was made in the image of thy Maker—not thy body, no—not thy mind, but thy *soul* was in the image of thy Creator. Then, it is the attuning of thy physical and mental attributes seeking to know the relationships to the Maker. *That* is true meditation. 281-41

Although most individuals in the West began hearing about meditation in the 1960s and 1970s, its practice has existed for thousands of years. For some, meditation is as natural as prayer. It is the practice of quieting our physical bodies and our minds, and focusing our attention inward instead of upon the material world around us. Meditation promotes coordination at three levels: physically, we begin to relax; mentally, our busied thoughts become quiet and we are able to become purposefully focused; and, spiritually, we can become attuned and reenergized to the presence of the Divine. Practically speaking, each of these levels enables us to deal both more effectively and more lovingly with the people and events with whom we come in contact.

Repeatedly, the readings advised individuals to work with both meditation and prayer. Although we may think of prayer as telling God what we need or want, Cayce believed that true prayer was not so much a petition for things as it was an expression of one's desire to gain an awareness of the Creator's will in our lives. In other words, prayer invites God to work through us. Meditation, on the other hand, is clearing aside all random thoughts so that we might become more attuned to the Divine. In the language of the readings, both are explained as follows:

For prayer is supplication for direction, for understanding. Meditation is listening to the Divine within. 1861-19

Then set definite periods for prayer; set definite periods for meditation. Know the difference between each. Prayer, in short, is appealing to the Divine within self, the Divine from without self, and meditation is keeping still in body, in mind, in heart, listening, listening to the voice of thy Maker. 5368-1

Although some schools of thought contend that the mind gets in the way of the meditator and must therefore be blanked out, the Cayce information suggests that whatever the mind dwells upon—whether in meditation or by the power of thought in general—becomes a greater portion of the individual's core: physically, mentally, and spiritually. In fact, when used constructively, the mind is a powerful tool which allows for a greater sense of relaxation and an awareness of the closest possible attunement. For that reason, the readings provided an affirmation for meditation which corresponds to each of the lessons in spirituality.

The creative potential of the human mind is so powerful, the first study group was told that an individual who focused upon spiritual things alone could become a "light unto the world" whereas an individual who focused only upon selfishness would literally become a "Frankenstein." For that reason, one's *intent* is extremely important when practicing meditation. Ultimately, that intent is to learn how to better express divine love in our interactions with one another. In addition, the readings suggested that one take the entire process of meditation seriously and remember it as a vehicle for cultivating our personal relationship with God:

Purify thy body. Shut thyself away from the cares of the world. Think on that as ye would do to have thy God meet thee face to face. "Ah," ye say "but many are not able to speak to God!" Many, you say, are fearful. Why? Have ye gone so far astray that ye cannot approach Him who is all merciful? He knows thy desires and thy needs, and can only supply according to the purposes that ye would perform within thine own self. Then, purify thy body, physically. Sanctify thy body, as the laws were given of old, for tomorrow the Lord would speak with thee—as a father speaketh to his children . . . Know that thy body is the temple of the living God. *There* He has promised to meet thee! 281-41

With this in mind, anyone can have a period of meditation by following a few simple steps. First, get into a comfortable position. It's probably best to sit in a chair, keeping your spine straight, your feet flat on the floor, and your eyes closed. Find a comfortable place for your hands, either in your lap or at your sides. In order to help with a balanced flow of energy throughout the physical body, the readings suggested keeping your palms down against your legs or closed against your stomach. Slowly take a few deep breaths and begin to relax. Breathe the air deep into your lungs, hold it for a moment, and then slowly breathe it out. With your mind, search your body for any obvious tension or tight muscles. You can try to relieve the tension by deep breathing, imagining the area is relaxed, or by gently massaging any tightness with your fingertips. When you have become comfortable and more at ease than when you first sat down, you are ready to move on. If you wish, the Cayce readings recommended a breathing exercise to assist in even greater levels of relaxation and attunement. Very simply, it is as follows:

First, breathe in slowly through the right nostril (covering the left nostril with your hand and keeping the mouth closed), then pinch your nostrils and breathe out through the mouth. Repeat this for a total of three times. Second, with your mouth closed, slowly breathe in through the left nostril (covering the right), then cover the left and breathe out through the right. Repeat this, as well, for a total of three times.

When your breathing exercise is complete, begin to focus your mind on one, single, peaceful, calming thought. Instead of thinking about what went on at work or what has to be accomplished with the remainder of your day, try focusing on a single thought such as "I am peaceful" or "I will be still and feel relaxed." You can also use a Bible verse (such as the Twenty-third Psalm or the Lord's Prayer) or a thought with a spiritual focus such as "God is Love." These thoughts are also called affirmations.

The first "stage" of actual meditation involves thinking about the message of your affirmation. In one of the examples cited above, you would think about the words *I am peaceful.* After a few moments of *thinking* the words, you should be able to move onto the second stage of meditation, which is *feeling* the meaning behind those words. For example, you could continue saying the words "I am peaceful"; however, the feeling behind these words can be much more meaningful than the actual words themselves.

In this second stage, try holding the feeling in silent attention, *without* needing the words of the affirmation. Gently bring your focus back to the words of the affirmation every time your mind begins to wander. That is to say, first begin thinking of the words of the affirmation, and then try to concentrate on the *feeling* behind them. Don't let yourself become discouraged when you find yourself thinking more about distractions than you are focusing upon the affirmation. It will take time to teach yourself to be able to think about only one thought. Spend anywhere from three minutes to fifteen minutes trying to hold the affirmation silently. These longer meditation periods will become natural after you've had some experience.

To end your meditation, consciously send out good thoughts or prayers to other people or situations in your life. It is at this point that you may wish to open your palms to enable the energy of meditation to flow through them. If you have been focusing upon peace, then try to send a sense of that peace to someone about whom you're concerned. As you begin to practice meditation daily it will become easier, and you might also notice that the sense of peace inside of you during meditation will begin to carry over into a greater portion of your day.

Sometimes certain physical sensations may occur in meditation: energy rising up the spine, gentle movements of the head and neck in a circular or side-to-side motion, etc. These sensations are simply a result of the movement of energy (often called the "kundalini" or even "spiritual energy") rising through the endocrine centers of your body: gonads, leydig, adrenals, thymus, thyroid, pineal, and pituitary.

Through the regular practice of meditation you can begin to heal yourself on many levels. As you focus upon a positive affirmation you may find that your negative habit-patterns will begin to change to be more in keeping with your positive affirmation. It is while practicing the silence of meditation, by relaxing your physical body and by quieting your conscious mind, that you can set aside your daily concerns for a moment and attempt to attune yourself to the spiritual side of who you really are. In fact, meditation is simply attuning the mind and the body to its spiritual source:

Meditation is *emptying* self of all that hinders the

creative forces from rising along the natural channels of the physical man to be disseminated through those centers and sources that create the activities of the physical, the mental, the spiritual man; properly done must make one *stronger* mentally, physically, for has it not been given? He went in the strength of that meat received for many days? Was it not given by Him who has shown us the Way, "I have had meat that ye know not of"? As we give out, so does the *whole* of man—physically and mentally become depleted, yet in entering into the silence, entering into the silence in meditation, with a clean hand, a clean body, a clean mind, we may receive that strength and power that fits each individual, each soul, for a greater activity in this material world. 281-13

As we take the time, each day, to put away from our thoughts the countless cares we seem bombarded with, we can begin to reestablish an awareness of our own spiritual nature. In one respect, prayer is talking to God, but meditation can be like listening to that portion of our being which is in constant communication with the Divine.

The most important relationship we all share is the one we have with God. In exploring that relationship, we come to know ourselves as well as our connectedness with one another. One of the most beneficial ways we can come to know that relationship is through the regular practice of meditation.

Note: At the beginning of each of the following twelve lessons you will find a MEDITATION AFFIRMATION designed to help you get the most out of the material. It is recommended that you memorize each affirmation and use it in your periods of meditation as you explore that lesson.

LESSON ONE

COOPERATION

Now there are diversities of gifts, but the same Spirit. And there are differences of administrations, but the same Lord. And there are diversities of operations, but it is the same God which worketh all in all. I Corinthians 12:4-6

MEDITATION AFFIRMATION

Not my will but Thine, O Lord, be done in me and through me. Let me ever be a channel of blessings, today, now, to those that I contact, in every way. Let my going in, my coming out be in accord with that Thou would have me do, and as the call comes, "Here am I, send me, use me." 262-3

COOPERATION

Introduction

The first lesson—as has been given—learn what it means to cooperate in one mind, in God's way; for, as each would prepare themselves, in meditating day and night, in "What wilt thou have me do, O Lord?" and the answer will *be* definite, *clear, to each . . . will they seek in His name . . . 262-1*

When individuals become interested in devoting more time and energy to personal spirituality, they may think about meditation, or prayer, or becoming more involved in their faith or a specific religion. Certainly, each of these activities can be extremely important in helping to bring an awareness of the Living Spirit into our lives. What may be surprising about the Edgar Cayce readings' approach to personal transformation is the fact that it suggests one of the first steps to really understanding our heritage as spiritual beings is through a lesson entitled "Cooperation."

Certainly, all of us think we know what the word *cooperation* means, and therefore too readily we may believe that there is nothing more to learn in this regard. It seems pretty apparent that we either know how to cooperate with another person or we don't. However, from Cayce's perspective, cooperation is not simply trying to *work with* another individual; rather, it is a *state of being* that sets aside personal agendas, motives, and desires so that God can use us as a "channel of blessings" to someone else. Perhaps more than anything else, this premise of somehow preparing ourselves for the activity of *Spirit* to flow through us is what defines the readings' approach to cooperation:

1

As it has so oft been given from the first, *know* that the Lord, thy God, is *one! Know* that thy ability, thy service, begins first with *cooperation* in *being* that channel through which the glory of the Lord may be manifested in the earth! 262-92

THE DYNAMICS OF COOPERATION

Individually and collectively we have a tremendous impact upon our present situation and our surroundings. When we interact with one another without a spirit of cooperation, we actually create disharmony in our lives and in our world. In other words, a non-cooperative attitude with just one other person affects the entire planet. Although at first this might be difficult to comprehend, as an analogy we can look at the human body. When any one part of the physical system is ill, or broken, or dis-eased, it actually affects the functioning of the whole. In the same manner, each of us is an integral part of the whole world and our thoughts, feelings, and activities have an impact upon all others. In the language of the readings:

Though there may be many approaches, cooperation in the activities—as in the Universe—brings the harmony of the universal activity; as does cooperation in human experience bring harmony and peace; while egotism and self-assertion and self-exaltation and self-indulgence bring inharmonious experiences, and the activities of turmoils, wars, strifes. 1297-1

By working with cooperation, we have the opportunity to positively affect all of materiality. The readings state that there are universal principles of harmony and unity that are trying to manifest into the third dimension. Even one person can make a difference. This manifestation is only possible through us as we attempt to become selfless channels through which the *spirit* can flow. Cooperation is a necessary step in bringing this about. Without cooperation, disharmony and chaos reign in our world environment. With cooperation, everything becomes possible. In fact, in one reading (262-4), the first study group was told that cooperation brings about harmony, and "harmony makes for peace; peace for understanding; understanding for enlightenment."

From Cayce's perspective, thoughts are as powerful as deeds in their creative potential. For this reason, both the mind and the body are necessary for true cooperation. Cooperation at the mental level deals with a unity of purpose. Cooperation at the physical level requires a harmony of activity. Cooperation within ourselves, as well as in our interactions with others, is necessary for the achievement of any outcome or for the attainment of any goal. We are told that "without that whole-hearted cooperation and oneness of mind and purpose, irrespective of position, condition, relation one with another, there may not be expected the result desired." (254-42) Therefore, true cooperation allows for a oneness of mind, a oneness of purpose, and a oneness of result. It allows for the manifestation of the Creator's laws and precepts in the earth—laws which are our natural heritage.

We are responsible for ourselves as well as for what we contribute to the whole. Every thought, every desire, every act that we put forth can't help but influence another—even someone on the other side of the world. Through cooperation we become aware of this interconnectedness with one another. True cooperation is not for the advantage of self, but rather for the advantage of the whole:

In cooperation *is* the offering of self to be a channel of activity, of thought; for as line upon line, precept upon precept, comes, so does it come through the giving of self; for he that would have life must *give* life, they that would have love must show themselves lovely, they that would have friends must be friendly, they that would have cooperation *must* cooperate by the *giving* of self *to* that as is to be accomplished—whether in the bringing of light to others, bringing of strength, health, understanding, these are one *in* Him. 262-3

In this regard, cooperation is not so much an activity of consensus as it is one of selflessness. It is not the demeaning of self, but rather purposefully choosing to use self as a channel of assistance to someone else. Ultimately, cooperation is best expressed through an attitude of loving service to others.

COOPERATION AS A PATTERN OF AWARENESS

There is within each one of us a pattern of perfection that is dormant, simply waiting to be awakened through the use of our own will. As we open our minds, our hearts, and our souls to becoming a channel of blessings, harmony, and cooperation, we naturally attune ourselves to this inner pattern of wholeness. From Cayce's perspective, this realization of wholeness was perhaps best exemplified in the life of Jesus, a child of God (just as we) who lost sight of himself and made his every thought and deed in harmony with the very best that was within him. By so doing, Jesus took on the "mind of Christ" and became the pattern of spiritual fulfillment for every soul in the earth. This Christ Consciousness was further described as "the awareness within each soul, imprinted in pattern on the mind and waiting to be awakened by the will, of the soul's oneness with God" (5749-14), and its manifestation is the eventual destiny of each and every soul.

Oftentimes, when individuals hear the terms "Christ" or "Jesus," right away they may arrive at preconceived notions based on their upbringing or particular religious background. Throughout history, the perspectives people have had on the life and teachings of Jesus have been varied, oftentimes even at odds. Some individuals involved in so-called "new age philosophies" or comparative religious studies have sometimes decided that Jesus was "just a teacher." *Was he only a prophet?* Others have decided to disregard him altogether. Members of non-Christian faiths may have ignored his life and ministry. *Was he a man who committed blasphemy by thinking himself a God?* Others may have said, "Well, Christians have been cruel to me and therefore I'm not interested in Jesus." Even among those who call themselves Christian there is no complete agreement about His divinity. Disagreements over the meaning of His life and ministry have resulted in dozens of denominational factions, charges of heresy or breaking away from the faith, and countless wars. *Was He the only son of God? Was He a God who became man, or always a God?* These and many other questions abound. However, the Edgar Cayce material offers a perspective that suggests there is a way of looking at Jesus' life in a manner that unifies humankind rather than divides us. In fact, for most of us, regardless of our religious background—whether we call ourselves Christian, or Jew, or Muslim, or Buddhist, or Hindu, or even agnostic—the Jesus we were brought up with is not necessarily the Jesus in the Edgar Cayce readings.

Essentially, the readings present Jesus as our "Elder Brother," a soul who came to show each one of us the way back to our spiritual Source by perfectly manifesting the laws of the Creator. Part of His mission was to demonstrate fully the living awareness of the spirit in the earth—something each one of us will eventually have to do. Ultimately, we will *all* be challenged to manifest that same pattern in our lives through service and unconditional love. Jesus' life of service to others provides an example for all of humankind. As one reading states:

> For the Master, Jesus, even the Christ, is the pattern for every man in the earth, whether he be Gentile or Jew, Parthenian or Greek. For all have the pattern, whether they call on that name or not; but there is no other name given under heaven whereby men may be saved from themselves. 3528-1

True cooperation, then, is allowing this consciousness of service—the same consciousness that was manifested in our Elder Brother, Jesus—to work through us. The readings called this putting on the mind of Christ:

> As we open our hearts, our minds, our souls, that we may be a channel of blessings to others, so we have the mind of the Christ, who took upon Himself the burden of the world. So may we, in our *own* little sphere, take upon ourselves the burdens of the world. The *joy*, the peace, the happiness, that may be ours is in *doing* for the *other* fellow. For, gaining an understanding of the laws as pertain to right living in all its phases makes the mind in attune with *Creative* Forces, which *are* of *His* consciousness. So we may have *that* consciousness, by putting into action *that* we know. 262-3

HOW MIGHT WE PUT
COOPERATION INTO ACTION?

Since true cooperation is choosing to become a channel of blessings to the world around us, how well are we doing? If we were to suddenly become aware of all the thoughts we hold in mind, do they most often create an atmosphere of peace, harmony, and understanding; or, do our thoughts give rise to anger, conflict, and disagreement? In our activities, how often do we remember to place another's needs before our own? Cultivating an awareness of our interactions with others is one of the best opportunities we can have to see our weaknesses as well as our strengths played out before our eyes. In fact, the readings state that each of us learns best about ourselves through our interactions with other individuals. Becoming aware of how well we are doing at attempting to manifest cooperation in our lives is an integral part of discovering *who* we are as well as *what* we need to learn.

Determine the aims and purposes. The purpose must be other than the glorifying of an individual's abilities, an individual's gifts, an individual's wishes or desires—but rather that individuals may become, through that cooperation of others, a greater channel for *blessings,* and the *blessings* coming from *God!* 254-57

In our relationships with others, whenever we choose to lose sight of our personal motives or selfish interests, cooperation can be the natural result. Cooperation is the consequence of awareness, service, self-sacrifice, and attunement. In fact, it may simply be the difference between looking for what we have in common rather than where we may differ. The common end that unites us all is our responsibility to one another. Interestingly enough,

Cayce believed that every person in our lives is there for a constructive reason—just as we are there for them:

> . . . be in the position of *fulfilling* the purposes whereunto one is dependent upon the other. For it is a unison of desire that brings a seeking at any time for expression, and *not* in *combative* reactions at all! For when there is the combative self-asser-tion, egotism and selfishness rise to the forefront *as* that ordinarily known as self-protection—which is a first law. But as long as there is kept that unison, correct—as long as there is that *great* activity which all should know. If the world will ever know its best, it must learn *cooperation!* 759-13

As we learn to express the best that is within us, giving others a sense of hope, a sense of peace, and a sense of understanding, we allow a portion of the Creative Forces to enter into their lives through us.

From a practical standpoint, if we are having difficulty with another individual, how might we best begin? Per-haps it can be as simple as replacing our negative thoughts with more positive ones. Have we ever stopped to think that even our own worst enemy has a best friend? What positive quality exists in the person that we've been somehow unable or unwilling to see? Instead of thinking unkindly about an individual with whom we've been having difficulty, let us instead discover if there is not something more positive to say. Perhaps we might go out of our way to show some small act of kind-ness to someone in need. What can we begin to do or to think that has somehow been neglected before? The readings' approach is to continually practice kind thoughts and actions toward even those who may have hurt us. Just as we desire to be treated (and thought of) by others, we need to begin dealing with those around us in the same manner. Only through this approach may we find the inner peace that comes with true cooperation.

For as has been given, do *today* that thou *knowest* to do, having little thought of the needs of the tomorrow, and on the morrow is given that ye have need of. How does He give? "Give us today our daily bread," not only the material but the mental and spiritual. "Direct me as I direct my fellow man, forgive me as I forgive." And thus we see cooperation, brotherly love, patience, long-suffering, gentleness, kindness, coming as *manifested* experiences into the hearts and minds and lives of others. And these are the fruits of the spirit of truth. Then as ye mete these day by day, ye find them becoming not only as stepping-stones for thine own self but the ladder of truth upon which others may climb. Ye cannot ask others, then, to do what ye would not do thyself. What ye propose, then, ye must *do*—in body, in mind, in spirit. 165-26

Through our own positive thought-processes we can put cooperation with others into action. Like begets like. If we would have friends, we must be friendly. If we wish to be loved, we must be loving. Whatever it is we wish to experience in our own life, we must be willing to give to others. If we would have harmony and cooperation in our experience, we must attempt to give them to someone else.

The entity should project self more in the way and manner of service to others, remembering that to become selfish, self-centered, self-satisfied, is belittling the Spirit that manifests within, for in cooperation with the Spirit from within may self be magnified, pacified, peacified, glorified! 2675-4

When the needs of others surpass the needs of self-ishness, cooperation will be the natural result. Our bodies and our minds will function more perfectly, because our intent will be for the good of the whole. The will of the Creator, which ever seeks to be manifested through His children, will find expression in the earth. In order to best cooperate:

> Do with all thy might what thy hand finds to do. Let *this* mind be in you as was in Him, "Not as I will but *Thine* will be done in earth as it is in heaven." Make thine self a channel of blessings to *someone;* so will His blessings come to thee, as an individual, as an integral part of the group. "They that seek my face shall find it." 262-3

True joy and happiness can only be found in service. Let us begin to seek the essence of cooperation that the Creator has placed within each one of us.

CONCLUSION

Regardless of what kind of cooperation we seek, physical, mental, or spiritual, action is necessary on our part to bring it about. In order to come together for a common cause, we must attempt to be united in our activity. We must begin to realize that another's need is at least as important as our own. In the physical or material world, cooperation is concurring with others in any action or effort. In the mental and spiritual worlds, it is setting aside our personal interests and becoming an aid to those around us. By being of assistance to someone else, by placing their needs before our own, we can experience cooperation in action. Whenever we help one another, we find ourselves functioning as "a channel of blessings." By so doing, we will bring joy and happiness to those around us, and will be manifesting God's love for His children in the earth.

Q. Is not cooperation a natural result when self is lost in the ideal?
A. This is a natural consequence of self-service, self-sacrifice, self-*bewilderment,* in Him. Being the channel is cooperation. Being a blessing is it in action. In whatever *state* of being, meet that upon the basis of *their* position—and *lift* up, look up—and *this* is cooperation. 262-3

Cooperation is the offering of self to be a channel of activity as well as of thought. In our daily lives we can take stock of our thoughts and our acts and begin to see whether our life is in alignment with the soul's desire for cooperation. This is not attained at once, but rather comes step by step, here a little, there a little, line upon line, precept upon precept. As we put into action all that we know of cooperation, through our thoughts and our deeds, by just being kind, by just being patient, by just being humble there will come to us an inner peace. Ultimately, we will gain the realization that true cooperation is simply being a channel of His blessings in the earth.

KNOW THYSELF

They are not of the world, even as I am not of the world.
John 17:16

MEDITATION AFFIRMATION

Father, as we seek to see and know Thy face, may we each, as individuals, and as a group, come to know ourselves, even as we are known, that we—as lights in Thee—may give the better concept of Thy Spirit in this world. 262-5

KNOW THYSELF

Introduction

What, then, is the purpose of the entering of a soul into material manifestations? In the beginnings, or in the activities in which the soul manifested individually, it was for the purpose of becoming as a companion of Creative Force or God; or becoming the whole body of God itself, with the ability—even as thy Pattern, as thy Savior, as thy Guide and Guard—to know thyself to be thyself, yet one with Him! That is the purpose for each entering into the material activities. 1650-1

Know thyself if ye would know thy God, if ye would be of a service to thy brother. 1256-1

One of the greatest challenges we may face as spiritual beings is the necessity of coming to know our true selves. Unfortunately, because we so often identify with our physical life, our personality, and our earthly experiences rather than our spiritual essence, reaching that objective can be challenging. The cares of life so frequently demand our entire focus that we might believe we don't have time to pursue anything else, let alone try to master spirituality. When this thought enters our minds, however, we need to remember that we are already spiritual beings. The challenge is not one of trying to become something else, instead it is an issue of not living up to the very best we already have within us.

The Cayce material confirms the fact that, too often, we forget our true nature. Many individuals have incorrectly assumed that our goal is to reach heaven, reach enlightenment, or simply "get out of the earth." And yet, this is looking at our heritage from a perspective quite different from that contained in the readings. The readings state that God desires to be expressed in the world through us—the example set by Jesus being the pattern for every soul. We are children of God with a mission to somehow bring *spirit* into the earth. One of the readings beautifully describes the spiritual nature of humankind in this way:

> For ye are as a corpuscle in the body of God; thus a co-creator with Him, in what ye think, in what ye do. And ye change each soul ye contact, literally or mentally—insofar as ye, as an individual entity, are a witness for or against thy Lord, thy God. This is the literal application, yea the spiritual way of man, of this entity in the earth; endowed, yes, with material attributes that to others may appear as a nonentity. Yet no soul may come in contact with the entity without being changed, either in body, in mind or in purpose. And purpose is, of course, of the soul. 2794-3

The truth about who we are is so monumental—we have an integral role in creating our lives, our experiences, our relationships, even world events! We have an effect upon every soul we encounter. The person who we truly are is vastly different from the way others see us or even from the way in which we see ourselves. Ultimately, we will come to know ourselves just as the Creator knows us.

THE TRIUNE NATURE OF HUMANKIND

One of the most frequently mentioned concepts in the Edgar Cayce material is that *Spirit is the life, mind is the builder, and the physical is the result.* In other words, *spirit* provides the creative impulse and energy in our lives. The *mind* focuses that energy into creative (positive) or destructive (negative) avenues of expression. The result of our interaction with the workings of spirit acted upon by the power of free will and the mind then becomes manifested into our lives. This suggests that all life has the capacity to be empowered by spirit, by the Creative Forces, by God. But the way in which we use that spiritual influence in our lives is determined by the power of our mind, by what we focus upon, by what we do with our free will. The impact of our choices will eventually find expression in the *physical,* affecting ourselves and our relationships with one another.

On one level, our physical bodies are material representations of the inner self seeking expression. Through our senses we become cognizant of the combined influences our positive and negative thoughts and actions have had upon us. Everything we have ever thought, acted upon, or desired will eventually have an effect upon the physical. In time, our magnified thoughts and desires become manifested into our physiognomy—registering in our very faces! Our physical bodies are composite units of the Creative Force, *spirit,* manifesting into the material world.

The way in which we focus the mind (the "mental body") is extremely important for it provides the inner self with either its greatest ally or its greatest adversary. It was for this reason that the apostle Paul advised his constituents to "Let this mind be in you, which was also in Christ Jesus . . . " (Philippians 2:5) What we continually focus upon becomes a greater part of our makeup as well as who we are in the process of becoming.

From Cayce's perspective, this process has been going on for ages. We are a composite of many more factors than simply chance, heredity, and environment. Each of us is a combination of such things as thoughts, desires, actions, choices, destiny, and even "karma" (karma being defined simply as *soul memory* and our own subconscious and conscious responses to that memory). Who we truly are *right now* is the result of everything that has influenced our individual development since our creation as souls.

We read in the Bible that "In my Father's house are many mansions." (John 14:2) This suggests that there are many states of consciousness beyond the physical and the ways in which we have interacted with all of these experiences have contributed to the sum total of who we are as individuals. Our physical, mental, and spiritual activities constantly affect our soul's ability to find expression in the material world. The soul draws to itself that which it has builded with its previous thoughts, desires, and actions. As we come to know ourselves, we will begin to realize that this cause-effect relationship ultimately enables us to understand every experience as a lesson in soul growth.

The spiritual counterpart of each of us (the "soul body") is a pattern of perfection that resides within us and is simply waiting for manifestation through our free will. This consciousness is greater than anything we have yet come to know about ourselves. However, rather than associating with this consciousness—our true self, or our spiritual *individuality*—we too often associate with our *personality*. In other words, our personality is what we show the world, whereas our individuality is who we really are—our true identity. From the readings' perspective, we are a far more dynamic creation than outward appearances might suggest. We possess physical, mental, and spiritual bodies which are constantly interacting with one another in an ongoing process of creation and soul development. The Cayce information further suggests that this triune nature of humankind is a symbolic representation of the entire cosmos. In the language of the readings:

Thus as you find in self body, mind, soul, in its three-dimensional manner it is as the spiritual three-dimensional concept of the Godhead; Father, Son, Holy Spirit. These, then, in self are a shadow of the spirit of the Creative Force. Thus as the Father is as the body, the mind is as the Son, the soul is as the Holy Spirit. 5246-1

Who we are in the present is a shadow of the Creative Forces at work. In other words, just as we are ultimately responsible for who we are right now, in our own little sphere of activity we are co-creators with God.

Are ye not all children of God? Are ye not co-creators with Him? Have ye not been with Him from the beginning? Is there any knowledge, wisdom or understanding withheld if ye have attuned thyself to that Creative Force which made the worlds and all the forces manifested in same? Thinkest thou that the arm of God is ever short with thee because thou hast erred? "Though ye be afar, though ye be in the uttermost parts, if ye call I will *hear!* and answer speedily." Thinkest thou that speakest of another, or to thee? Open thy mind, thy heart, thy purpose to thy God and His purpose with thee. 294-202

OUR HERITAGE AS CO-CREATORS

It is important to remember that we are not physical bodies with souls, but are rather souls, children of the Creator, who are manifesting in the material world. In one respect, the physical body is simply the house, the home of the soul, during its sojourn in materiality. Though we often think of ourselves as a body, the body is simply the vehicle for mental and spiritual expression.

The .physical body allows the spirit to experience the confines of a limited dimension as well as the dynamics of free will, choice, decision, and cause and effect.

As a co-creator, we need to become serious about the role we play in creating the world around us. We need to begin recognizing our personal responsibility. In fact, unless we begin responding to life as *conscious co-creators*, we are actually contributing to global problems and personal difficulties:

> For, know that each soul is a free-willed individual, and chooses the way and the application. For it is either the co-worker with God in creation— and creative then in its attitude, in its thought, in its application of tenets and truths day by day; *or* in attune with that which is at variance, and thus besetting or putting stumbling blocks in the way of others along the way. 2549-1

> The Creator intended man to be a companion with Him. Whether in heaven or in the earth or in whatever consciousness, a companion with the Creator. How many [lifetimes/experiences] will it require for thee to be able to be a companion with the Creative Forces wherever you are? 416-18

Cayce's approach to our co-creative abilities is one which constantly builds for the future. Regardless of our present circumstance, regardless of current world events, regardless of how overwhelmed we may feel right now, the readings state:

> . . . ye can do something about it! For know that ye are in the present experience, in the present environ, in the present years of thy activity more productive, more far-reaching in the influence ye

have, in the opportunity that ye will have for making the earth a better place to live in for those to
come. And remember you'll be back again! What do
you want it to look like? . . . you'd better be up and
doing . . . 4047-2

What do we want the world to look like? Right now we
can begin to respond consciously to life as a co-creator.
We can begin to realize that we are every bit responsible
for shaping the course of our lives. We can begin to see
our lives and the status of human affairs as merely a reflection of what we need to work on, as well as what we
are (and are not) doing to help create the future around
us.

KNOWING OURSELVES THROUGH OTHERS

It may come as a surprise, but one of the leading ideas
contained within the Cayce readings is that it is through
others that we most often come to know ourselves.
Whether it is through learning about love in the face of a
child, or growing in patience through our experiences
with a friend, it is through our interactions with others
that we become aware of our shortcomings, our faults,
our abilities, and our talents. It is through our encoun-
ters with others that we come to realize what we need to
work on, as well as what it is with which we have to work.
It is through other people that we grow in our awareness
of our relationship with God and come to know ourselves.

According to the readings, there is an undergirding
dynamic in every human relationship—a *universal
law*—which is described as "Like attracts like." What this
means is that everything we put out through thought or
deed comes back to us. This should not really come as a
surprise when we consider our co-creative abilities in

creating our environment. What may be challenging, however, is the idea this suggests: *we can see our own strengths and weaknesses in other people:*

> Remember—these are as the unchangeable laws: As ye mete to others, it comes back to thee. As ye would that others should do to thee, do ye even so to them. This applies whether in family or in just acquaintance, or associates of any kind. Know that the fault ye find in others is a reflection of a fault in thyself. Be to others just as you would have others be to thee, and ye will remove much of that. *Do not* hold the idea, "Well, I know what they are going to say or do, but I'll do as best I can." Disregard that! *know* the spirit with which *ye* do a thing is the spirit that will respond to thee! 1688-9

Cayce stated that individuals in our environment literally act as a mirror. The people in our life who may be the most frustrating to us, are frustrating because we are seeing in them a portion of ourselves that we have somehow overlooked or refused to deal with. Conversely, the people in our life that we truly admire are showing us a reflection of some quality we can utilize within ourselves. Although this concept might be difficult to believe at first, all one need do is to remember that *even my own worst enemy has a best friend, and even my best friend has someone who doesn't like them.* Why? The answer has to do with the focus of our perception.

Each of us is drawn to perceiving specific traits in individuals for a reason. In fact, whenever we have an emotional response to another person (positively or negatively) we can be certain that there is something more for us to learn. If we want to see what we need to work on spiritually, we need to look around at the people in our lives that drive us crazy. If we want to see what we have to work with, we need to look around at the people whom we truly admire. In this manner, we will begin to see our own strengths and weaknesses portrayed in others. Becoming aware of this dynamic can give us an entirely different attitude about all of humankind:

> For the first law is, "Like begets like." And what ye sow, ye shall reap. It is, then, how ye mete that ye reap in thine relationships one to another . . . Then, the first law of knowing self, of understanding self, is to become more and more sincere with that thou doest in the relationships one to another. For the proof of same is the fruit thereof. And when thou hast found the way, thou showest the way to thy brother. 261-15

Personal reflection can be a powerful tool for coming to know oneself. Thinking back over the words and the activities of each day we might ask ourselves: Why did I do this or that? Am I expressing the concepts of what I say (or think) I believe in my interactions with others? Would I have acted in front of someone I truly respect (perhaps even my Creator!) in the same manner that I acted toward a particular individual I don't like? From the soul's perspective, every person in the earth is my sister and my brother—am I treating them as such? We must remember that, in part, the people in our life hold the key to the process of our own growth and development:

> Q. *What must I do in order to know self better?*
> A. As self meditates upon the various activities of self, as to how oft self becomes the impetus of another's activity, then there may be seen that self is understood, or *not* understood, as the *activities* of self have been. How oft in thine own self has *thou*

been that, that *impelled* another to look within themselves as to whether they were in accord with that *He* would have them do? How *oft* hast thou made another think better of themselves? Not *laud* themselves, but think *better* of themselves? In this may one see self; for in magnifying Him self sees self as *others* may see self in self's activities. 262-9

As we lose sight of our selfish interests in relationship to others we will be able to tap into that portion of our individuality that desires to be whole, that portion that desires true self-expression, that portion that desires to come to know itself.

AWAKENING TO OUR TRUE SELF

In many ancient cultures there was the belief that God placed all knowledge of our true relationship with the Creator deep inside of us, and yet, this is often the last place that individuals decide to look. The truth of our divine nature is clearly illustrated in a popular Hindu legend:

At one time all men on earth were gods, but men so sinned and abused the Divine that Brahma, the god of all gods, decided that the godhead should be taken away from man and hid in some place where he would never again find it and abuse it. "We will bury it deep in the earth," said the other gods. "No," said Brahma, "because man will dig down in the earth and find it." "Then we will sink it in the deepest ocean," they said. "No," said Brahma, "because man will learn to dive and find it there, too." "We will hide it on the highest mountain," they said. "No," said Brahma, "because man will some day climb every mountain on earth and again capture the godhead." "Then we do not know where to hide it where he cannot find it," said the lesser gods. "I will tell you," said Brahma, "hide it down in man himself. He will never think to look there."

The Bible confirms this same idea when it states:

For this commandment which I command thee this day, it is not hidden from thee, neither is it far off. It is not in heaven, that thou shouldest say, Who shall go up for us to heaven and bring it unto us, that we may hear it and do it? Neither is it beyond the sea, that thou shouldest say, Who shall go over the sea for us, and bring it unto us, that we may hear it, and do it? But the word is very nigh unto thee, in thy mouth, and in thy heart, that thou mayest do it. Deuteronomy 30:11-14

The readings describe this awareness as the Christ Consciousness—a pattern of perfection which is whole and is in harmony with our spiritual essence. Through a process of both attunement and application, we begin to manifest that spiritual consciousness. In addition to meditation and prayer, working with our dreams can be an integral part of personal discovery and inner attunement. There are many books available on the subject, but one of the most important first steps is to simply begin writing them down each morning. In terms of application, overall progress is perhaps best seen through our ongoing interactions with others.

As we come to know our true individuality, we will discover our connectedness with one another. We'll begin to recognize the fact that with God as our Parent, we are all children of the same family. We will discover that part of us that has always been whole:

... the first awareness of which each soul should
become cognizant or seek earnestly, is that God is
conscious of thee. And the very fact of your own
awareness should ever remind thee of this. If each
soul would or could become aware of that, how
much difference there might be in the choices
made day by day! 2650-1

More and more frequently we awaken to our true
spiritual self as we become conscious of the fact that God
is aware of us, that He is mindful of our activities, and
that His Spirit is within us as well as without. This is the
essential purpose for coming to know oneself.

CONCLUSION

Each of us is a manifestation of all that we have ever
been. As we come to know ourselves, we will discover
that who and where we are *right now* is simply the end
result of our previous thoughts, desires, and actions. And
yet, in spite of any challenges, disappointments, or
shortcomings we may face, we each possess a pattern
for wholeness which is our birthright. Every aspect of our
lives: physically, mentally, and spiritually, has the potential to contribute toward the realization and manifestation of this pattern. All experiences have the potential,
ultimately, to be for our own growth and good, for they
assist us in coming to know ourselves. As we become attuned to our true inner selves, our daily lives will exemplify the best that is within us and we will finally be
worthy to call ourselves Children of God:

Know thyself first. Look within thine own heart.
What is it ye would purpose to do? Satisfy thine own
appetites? Satisfy thine own desire for power or
glory, for fame or fortune? These, as ye have experi-

enced and as ye know within thy deeper self, easily take wings and fly away. Only those things that are just, those things that are beautiful, those things that are harmonious, that arise from brotherly kindness, brotherly love, patience, hope and graciousness, *live.* 1776-1

In order to be true to others, we must first be true to that inner part of ourselves. We can't say one thing and yet be and think something entirely differently. As we cultivate this ability to discriminate between right and wrong, good and bad, what we really believe versus what we let others think we believe, even where we want to be versus where we are, we become more completely aware of the motivation of our thoughts, our desires, and our activities. We become aware of where it is our life is leading us and whether or not we need to make a change. But most importantly, we become aware of the potential for wholeness simply waiting to be awakened within ourselves.

We are co-creators with God. Only the application of spiritual principles such as patience, cooperation, tolerance, and love will lead to this awareness and our own spiritual awakening. Through our interactions with others we come to know ourselves, our relationship with one another, and our relationship with our God:

Would ye act before thy God in the manner ye act before thine brother? Love one another. "A new commandment I give, that ye *love* one another." In *this* manner may each see themselves as others see them. Let not thy words and thy actions be so different that they are not children of the same family. Let thy deeds, let thy words, be in keeping with that others see in thee. 262-9

We must challenge ourselves to be willing to begin measuring ourselves against that standard of love. We must begin treating others just as we ourselves would wish to be treated. It is our duty, even our obligation, to discipline ourselves so that our every word, thought, and action begins to reflects the very best that we have within us.

LESSON THREE

IDEALS

Let this mind be in you, which was also in Christ Jesus . . .
Philippians 2:5

MEDITATION AFFIRMATION

God, be merciful to me! Help Thou my unbelief! Let me see in Him that Thou would have me see in my fellow man. Let me see in my brother that I see in Him whom I worship! 262-11

IDEALS

Introduction

Then, the more important, the most important experience of this or any individual entity is to first know what is the ideal — spiritually. 357-13

All of us, at different periods in our lives, struggle with what we should be doing, where we should be going, or how we might possibly fill that special niche which God has in mind for us. We find ourselves searching for something, although we often remain unsure as to what it is. Since this state of inner confusion is something we all have in common, you would think that any practical solution that provided insights or addressed an answer to this dilemma would be heralded from the highest mountain peak. Yet, perhaps one of the most frequently overlooked principles in the Edgar Cayce readings is the concept of working with "ideals," and it's that very same principle that can provide us with an approach to answering this inner call.

> For, mental and spiritual guidance should be related to what an individual entity chooses as its ideal, and what it will or should do about that ideal, not ideas but ideals. In choosing and in analyzing self and the ideal, do not merely carry these in mind but put them, as it were, upon the paper in a manifested form. 5091-3

Because the readings recommend writing down our ideals, physically, mentally, and spiritually, we may be tempted to believe this approach is one in which we complete a one-time assignment, filling in columns or jotting down notes that are never again wrestled with once set on paper. And yet, Cayce made it clear that the importance of working with ideals should become a frequent activity in our lives—one in which we're challenged, encouraged, even prodded to begin a personal masterpiece at a soul level. From this approach, the readings' insights on ideals can provide much assistance in helping us to manifest in our lives the very best we have to offer our world, our God, and ourselves.

JUST WHAT IS AN IDEAL?

In simplest terms an ideal is the motivating influence that undergirds the intentionality of *why* we do what we do. It is like a North Star that guides us in the dark of night, allowing us to focus upon the direction in which we wish to be headed. Whereas a "goal" is something attainable, in Cayce's terminology an "ideal" is really a motivating pattern that guides our lives. It's not something we're going to gather up like a prized object; rather, it's more like facing into the sun—the rays warm our face as we look toward it and we can't help but know when we're looking straight at it!

What may be surprising from the readings perspective, however, is that everyone works with ideals, even if it is at an unconscious level. For example, one person was told, "Each individual entity, whether aware of same or not, sets before self an ideal in the material world, in the mental world, in the spiritual world." (1011-1) Another individual was told that the reason he had so many problems and so much confusion in his own life was because he had never really established a *conscious* ideal (323). He often felt like he was in a state of confusion simply because the ideal he had established (to be sure, unconsciously) was that of a "wanderer." He was encouraged to make a conscious choice and to begin working with it in a positive way. The readings frequently reminded individuals that "Mind is the builder"; in other words, what an individual dwells upon becomes a greater part of his or her life.

The readings suggest that one way to begin discovering what kind of unconscious ideals we've been constructing in our own lives is to ask ourselves introspective questions like the following: (1) What sort of workplace would my company be if every employee were just like myself? (2) What sort of home life would there be if every wife/husband/child were just like myself? (3) What sort of neighborhood would this be if every neighbor were just like myself? (4) What sort of self-worth would individuals have if every person had my self-esteem? or, (5) What sort of church or synagogue would my congregation be if every member were just like myself? Questions like these aren't meant to discourage us but instead to help us realize just how powerful unconscious ideals have been in shaping what we've become, both positively and negatively.

A conscious ideal is one with which we are willing to measure our every thought, word, and deed. For example, if we chose a conscious ideal such as "love," it should establish our criterion for our every action. It could also point us in the *direction* we wish to be headed. Using the five questions above in conjunction with an ideal of love, we might ask ourselves: (1) What sort of an employee would a loving person be? (2) What kind of a home life would a loving person have? (3) What sort of a neighbor would a loving person be like? (4) How might a loving person exhibit self-worth and self-esteem? or (5) What would a loving member of a church or a synagogue be like? By discovering our "best guesses" as to the qualities of a loving person (or whatever quality we've currently chosen for our ideal), we can begin to exhibit those same qualities in ourselves and in the process begin to demonstrate more of the ideal we wish to have motivating our every action.

So, in answer to our question "What is an ideal?"—it is something that influences our every act, our every thought, even all of our emotions. It is a motivating impulse shaping the substance of who we are, as well as who we eventually become. As powerful a motivator as ideals are in our lives, unless we become cognizant of them and take the initiative, they can remain largely unconscious. We may actually have ideals and not even know what they are!

So why are ideals important? In part, the answer to the *what* establishes the *why*. Since ideals shape our very lives, our experiences, even who we are in the process of becoming, they must be extremely important. The readings themselves state that setting a conscious ideal is the single most important thing we can accomplish. Essentially, the reason for this importance is threefold: (1) ideals direct and shape the impulse of "spirit" in our lives; (2) ideals help us deal with (and hold us accountable to) those experiences we need in order to come to know ourselves; and (3) ideals can help us work through the sometimes-confusion we've come to call "freedom of choice."

IDEALS DIRECT AND SHAPE THE IMPULSE OF SPIRIT IN OUR LIVES

The entire (oft-repeated) quote from the Cayce material regarding "mind is the builder" is as follows: *Spirit is the life; mind is the builder; and the physical is the result.* Although vastly simplifying the terminology, the word "spirit" in the readings vocabulary is really the Creative Impulse that can be utilized positively or negatively. It is the life-force that can be directed through the activity of the mind and will for selfless (good) or selfish (evil) pursuits. The mind is the mechanism through which we decide where and how we will focus our creative energies, even our attention. The end result of focusing this creative impulse in a specific direction or activity (consciously or unconsciously) is that we draw certain experiences, even people, into our lives. *In fact, our physical/material world becomes the stage (the result) upon which we can see the activity of spirit, directed through the power of our own minds, played out before our very eyes.*

From the readings:

> For whatever there may be is first conceived in spirit. It is acted upon by mind. Dependent, then, upon what the mind of the entity holds as its ideal, or as to what form or manner it would give give by and through what spirit it would build in its mental self. 2995-3

This same individual was told in her reading: "Ye can make thyself just as happy or just as miserable as ye like."

How many of us have ever walked into a multi-screen movie theater without even looking at the marquee or having a sense of what was being shown, purchased a ticket for whatever show the attendant happened to feel like selling us, and then simply sat down without even caring what it was we were going to watch? And yet, this is the very experience we create for ourselves when we don't make the commitment to establish a conscious ideal.

IDEALS HELP US DEAL WITH (AND HOLD US ACCOUNTABLE TO) THOSE EXPERIENCES WE NEED IN ORDER TO COME TO KNOW OURSELVES

Once an ideal has been chosen it sets in place a pattern, a motivating influence, that will assist us in learning whatever lesson it is we need in order to move toward that next step leading to our personal growth and development. Complicating our understanding, however, is the fact that once an ideal has been chosen our life sometimes draws experiences seemingly diametrically opposed to what it is we said we were interested in building.

For example, working with an ideal of "love," if we decided that we needed to be more loving in our lives we might soon discover that we were suddenly surrounded by individuals who were either unloving themselves or a real challenge to try to love. This experience would not mean that we had chosen the wrong ideal; rather, it would simply indicate that we were drawing toward us individuals and events that would help us learn how to become more loving. Ultimately, the only way we can experience real learning at a soul level is by our interaction, connection, and service to one another. The readings challenge us not to give up on the ideal we have chosen once the real work begins. We're accountable for our choices, and we'll see some results if we stick with them.

This is the . . . unfaltering principle . . . the law— *love* . . . forsake *not* these principles . . . thou dost set as an ideal! Be *patient* and . . . thy efforts . . . will not go unrewarded . . . 802-2

IDEALS CAN HELP US WORK THROUGH THE SOMETIMES-CONFUSION WE'VE COME TO CALL "FREEDOM OF CHOICE"

Ideals can be wonderful tools for making decisions. Whenever we find ourselves in a state of confusion because we're unable to make a choice, whether it's a major decision such as a change in careers or a relatively unimportant decision such as how to spend the afternoon, our ideal can help. Simply weigh each choice against the ideal; for example, if our ideal is "love" and we are suddenly presented with the unbelievable prospect of two job opportunities at the same moment in time, we might ask ourselves which one of these jobs is most in keeping with what a loving person would do or which one of these would help an individual become more loving?

But more than helping us to make simple choices, our ideals can lead us out of the confusion of what we should be doing, or where we should be going, or even what God would have us do with our lives. The ideal helps guide us toward the next meaningful step in our spiritual journey. Two oft-repeated quotes from the readings are "line upon line, precept upon precept" and "do what ye know to do and the next step will be given." As we begin working with whatever understanding we possess, our path is made clear:

For as ye apply day by day that ye know, then is the next step, the next act, the next experience shown thee. 262-104

THE APPLICATION OF
IDEALS IN DAILY LIFE

The challenge of working with ideals seems to be one where we're encouraged to move beyond simply a personal intellectual exercise to one where we're able to strategically map out how our ideal will affect our interactions with others, ourselves, even our surroundings:

First, know thy ideal—spiritually, mentally, materially. Not so much as to what you would like others to be, but what may be *your* ideal relationships to others! For he that is the greatest is the servant of all—as the law of cause and effect.1998-1

Many individuals have found that the key to making a spiritual ideal practical in their material lives is to again work with the idea that: "Spirit is the life; mind is the builder; and the physical is the result." The readings spelled it out as follows:

Write *physical.* Draw a line, write *mental.* Draw a line, write *spiritual.*

Put under each, beginning with the *spiritual,* (for all that is in mind must first come from a spiritual concept) what is thy spiritual concept of the ideal, whether it be Jesus, Buddha, mind, material, God or whatever is the word which indicates to self the ideals spiritual.

Then under the *mental* heading write the ideal mental attitude, as may arise from concepts of the spiritual, in relationship to self, to home, to friends, to neighbors, to thy enemies, to things, to conditions.

Then write what is thy ideal spiritual, mental, material [physical]. What is the ideal *material,* then?

Not of conditions but what has brought, what does bring into manifestation the spiritual and mental ideals. What relationships does such bring to things, to individual, to situations?

Thus an individual entity analyzes itself. Then set about to apply the knowledge ye have attained, for ye will get ideas and that ideal. Ye may change them from period to period, as ye study them over. For as ye apply them they become thy ideals. To be just as theories they do not belong to thee, they are still theories so far as thy personal being is concerned. It's the application of same that counts. What do they bring into thine experience? These are well if ye will apply them. 5091-3

Simply stated, the first step entails taking a sheet of paper and drawing three columns. Label the first "My Spiritual Ideal," label the second "My Mental Attitudes," and label the third "My Physical Activities." Although we're encouraged to choose a *challenging* spiritual ideal, it's recommended that the spiritual ideal we choose be something we can understand, work with, and see progressively manifested in our lives.

The Cayce material suggests that, ultimately, a spiritual ideal is the highest "spiritual" quality or attainment that we could hope to have motivating us in our lives right now. For some, this might be the pattern set by Jesus, for others it might be a quality such as "love." In order to really begin working with ideals, however, we should choose that quality or attribute that is currently missing or lacking in our own life in our relationships with others. For example, perhaps we may find that we need to be more "patient" or more "forgiving" or more "understanding" in our interaction with other people. Ideals grow and change as we do, so it's important to pick something with which we can really begin to work.

For this exercise, let's say that our spiritual ideal is currently going to be "forgiveness," so forgiveness would be written under the first column labeled "My Spiritual Ideal."

Under the second column, we need to begin listing "My Mental Attitudes"—those *attitudes* which will help build that spirit of forgiveness into our relationships with others and with ourselves. Perhaps we'll decide "compassion" is an attitude we will work toward in a frustrating relationship with a parent; maybe "openness" is the mental attitude we want to begin holding in regard to one of our children with whom we've been having difficulty; and possibly "patience" best describes that attitude we need to use with ourselves. Our ideals' chart should list all the people in our lives with whom we need to exercise this spiritual ideal of forgiveness, plus a positive mental attitude suggesting how we will begin working with each one.

The third column is the most detailed. It's the one place we can write out all those physical *activities* we'll begin doing in relationship to specific individuals. "My Physical Activities" should simply reflect the mental attitudes we're holding in relationship to our spiritual ideal. For example, with the case of ourselves and the mental attitude of "patience," perhaps each of the following would be appropriate activities to help build that same attitude: "stop saying (or even thinking) 'I can't,' " "make a list of every instance where I have been forgiven for something," "begin praying that I will have the determined endurance to go forward," etc. Each attitude and person should have next to it a list of multiple activities with which we'll be working. These activities should map out ways to bring the spiritual ideal into the material world.

We'll know that progress has been made with our spiritual ideal when the mental attitude listed on the ideals sheet becomes our usual state of mind, and our physical activity becomes our automatic and natural response. As we really begin to work with ideals, making them a part of who we are, we can then choose a more challenging direction—a brighter North Star toward which we can point our lives. The important thing is to *work* with our ideals, for by working with them we'll discover what it is we should be doing. Then we no longer have to concern ourselves with the timing:

> Wherever you are! Whether in Hartford or Sing Sing, or Kalamazoo or Timbuktu, it's one and the same! The Lord is God of the universe, wherever thou art! For each soul finds self in that place which it occupies in the present only by the grace of God. Then use that today, that period. If it is used properly, then the next is pointed out. 3356-1

IDEALS CHANGE AND GROW AS WE DO

As we work with ideals we will discover that they need to be fine-tuned, becoming even more challenging with the passage of time. For example, if one of our ideals is "gentleness of speech" we would continue to work with it—even across the breakfast table—until it became a part of us. Once our conversation began to match up with "gentleness of speech" we might reword our ideal to "friendliness." Then, "friendliness" would be the spiritual ideal we'd attempt to manifest in our experiences with others in our mental attitudes and our physical activities. Eventually, we might find that we've grappled with "gentleness of speech," "friendliness," and a dozen others all dealing with some aspect of "service" or "improving relationships" or "unconditional love." For each one of our smaller ideals is a portion of something greater that we wish to become, but is perhaps out of our reach in the very beginning.

ULTIMATELY, THERE IS ONE IDEAL

Although the readings encourage us to choose a personal ideal, they also assert that there is only one Ideal. One individual was told "There is *one* way, but there are many paths." (3083-1) In essence, what this suggests is that each of us is moving toward an ultimate Ideal. Whether we want to label that ideal "perfection" or "Christ Consciousness" or "God Consciousness" or whatever term with which we're personally comfortable, the ultimate ideal is the highest spiritual attainment possible. Therefore, each of our smaller ideals (such as aspects of "love" or "service" or "kindness") really serve as steps or building blocks toward that highest ideal. Interestingly enough, it is this ultimate ideal that Cayce claimed was written upon the very fiber of the soul—a consciousness described as the awareness of the soul's oneness with God (5749-14).

CONCLUSION

A conscious ideal enables us to establish an appropriate *why* behind our activities. It gives us a structure for discernment with which we can work in daily life. When we attempt to live without bringing a spiritual motivation into everyday awareness, we may feel as though we are simply drifting without a clear direction. Without an ideal, we have the very real possibility of simply becoming motivated by our desires, our fears, and our habit patterns. We may fail to live up to the very best within us:

> . . . until there is the consciousness in the experience of the individual that the very act of living is the expression of the Creative Forces or God, and thus what the individual does with its opportunities of making that expression in line with his ideal

or concept of the God he would worship—it isn't worthwhile. 1210-2

Repeatedly, the readings encourage us to become aware of what we are building within ourselves, because ultimately we will have to meet it. As we work with a conscious ideal, not only is our direction made more clear, but the ideal becomes a living, breathing portion of who we are at a soul level. An ideal is like a personal tapestry that we create one stitch at a time. It can be worked with and ironed out and toiled over until the end result is something we can proudly share in our interactions with others. Each of us has the opportunity to consciously decide who we wish to become as well as how long it's going to take us to get there.

Although each of us might have different ideas, plans, or goals about *how* things should be done, the readings advise that—in spite of all our differences—we can share a common *why*. Even during the turmoil and international chaos of the 1930s, the readings gave a type of prescription that could serve to bring all of humanity together. In spite of the fact that each nation had different ideas, Cayce suggested that the world could share a common ideal. That ideal was his "answer to the world":

The world, *as* a world . . . has lost its ideal. Man may not have the same *idea*. Man—*all* men—may have the same *ideal!* . . . that can only come with all having the one Ideal; not the one idea, but "Thou shalt love the Lord thy God with all thine heart, thy neighbor as thyself!" This [is] the whole law, this [is] the whole answer to the world, to each and every soul. That is the answer to the world conditions as they exist today. 3976-8

FAITH

Now faith is the substance of things hoped for, the evidence of things not seen.   Hebrews 11:1

MEDITATION AFFIRMATION

Create in me a pure heart, O God! Open Thou mine heart to the faith Thou hast implanted in all that seek Thy face. Help Thou mine unbelief in my God, in my neighbor, in myself! 262-13

FAITH

Introduction

Faith, as has been defined by Barnabas, is the substance of things hoped for . . . Hence, as has been termed by many, that faith—pure *faith—accepting or rejecting without basis of reason, or* beyond *the ken or scope of that as is perceived through that that man brings to his own activity through that of his five senses . . . 262-14*

. . . for without faith none may gain the highest development in the material or the spiritual plane; for when one may not have faith in that not seen, how may one expect that reflected from self to inspire others to faith in that the body-mind, the mental-mind, or the self represents? 369-3

Faith, perhaps more than anything else, is an attribute of the soul that allows God's spirit to work through us. It is an energetic force that provides a pathway through which the Creative Forces can manifest. In part, it is a motivation that undergirds the attitudes of openness, trust, discipline, and hope, but it is much more. It is an inner quality that can be cultivated and expressed in our every action and our every thought. Though faith is not related to knowledge, it is an extraordinary way of knowing. It is a force that makes possible the bridging of the seen with the unseen. It is the substance which lays the foundation for the direction of our lives. Most importantly, faith is an inner awareness of the soul's relationship with its Creator.

The Cayce readings suggest that sometimes in our daily lives we may mistake confidence for faith. However, the two are not the same. Confidence relates more to the material world—such as a belief in a thing or an outcome. In this respect, confidence may be regarded as an outgrowth of knowledge. It is also most often associated with an attitude regarding one's self, whereas faith suggests that one is in partnership with God. Faith blossoms and grows as we do. It is like the energy of love which can empower our interactions with another. In simplest terms, an attitude of open-trust might be seen as a faint glimmer of that which is real faith. In fact, Cayce stated that as we cultivate our trust in God, one's growing faith would be the natural result.

Too often throughout the history of the world, humankind has associated faith with religious dogma, belief, ritual or even culture. In actuality, each of these is associated with the holding of certain ideas, and faith is none of these things. Faith is an inner awareness, sparked by the soul, that may be brought into consciousness through service. Faith is the dynamic that allows the energy of spirit to work through us in spite of our imperfections. Faith is that which has brought into manifestation all that has ever existed and all that could ever be conceived to exist. Faith is the evidence of God's promises fulfilled.

More than anything else, faith is an awareness to be lived rather than a thing to behold.

FAITH AS A UNIVERSAL FORCE

Because faith is not the belief in a thing but rather a soul awareness longing to be expressed, the existence of faith is true for every individual. To be sure, some may be unaware of the faith which abides within their being, but regardless, the activities of the spirit may flow through them to the same level they desire to be of assistance to another. Faith can neither be destroyed nor totally absent. It is not of the physical, it is of the soul. In

fact, from the readings perspective, faith is that which
puts into action the very best that an individual has
come to know:

> . . . as given, faith is the essence of creative forces
> within the active force of that of an individual to
> which they apply themselves in the spiritual activ-
> ity of their experience. So, in the application of that
> known to self as an expression of that faith as is
> manifest in every child of God—that in its active
> force puts that known into operation—does this
> grow, expand, or *become* the basis *of* the activities
> of self in those directions as necessary. 262-17

From this perspective, any activity, service, good work,
ethic, or desire to be of aid has its foundation in faith.
Therefore, the essence of faith itself provides for the
manifestation of all that is good.

True faith is exercised whenever the conscious mind
brings to its awareness from the inner self some aspect
of wholeness, and this awareness is, in turn, acted upon
through the activity of service, of spiritual forces, of love.
It is in this way that each of us may come to know our
inner self, our very soul, through the exercising of faith.
More and more, as individuals awaken to their true spiritual nature, the awareness and force of faith becomes
available for practical everyday use:

> For there is the call deep within self for service.
> This the entity, then, would apply. To be sure, there
> must be faith irrespective of works, but faith with-
> out works is dead, or it bears little relationship. For,
> activity of spirit in the earth is not a latent but a very
> positive fact, as was indicated in the life of the Mas-
> ter in the earth. For each day, each period was filled
> with activities until it could be written of Him "I

suppose that all books in the world would not hold all the doings or sayings of this man." 3361-1

In practical terms, an individual's faithfulness is realized whenever they act upon the very best they have come to know in this time, in this place, right now. However, regardless of our present state of mind, faith exists as a potential awareness upon the very fiber of our being.

FAITH AS A GROWING AWARENESS

According to the Edgar Cayce material, the full realization of our spiritual growth ultimately rests upon the development of our faith. Faith is not something which can be taught; rather it is an awareness that can only be cultivated within one's self. Faith goes beyond belief and trust; it is a stretching of one's consciousness. Faith allows us to experience and to know the unseen dimensions of life regarding higher truths about the soul. For this reason, working with a spiritual motivation or ideal is a necessary step in the unfoldment of one's faith:

For as the man thinketh in his heart, so is he. Then, if ye would not be condemned, condemn not. If ye would have faith, *show* faith. If ye would have love, show love. Yea—ye say, "This I have heard so oft!" Yes, but what have you done about it? Ye must realize, then, that God *is*—and thy body is the temple of thy God! Do ye meet Him there? 254-101

Hence the necessity as is in the entity's whole experience, that the faith, that hope in a divinity that is *within* be held—that shapes the destinies of individual experiences in such a way that the opportunities that come into the lives of individuals are those things which if taken correctly make for the greater soul development. 1300-1

The full experience of faith is not possible without a disciplined focus of one's inner vision on a spiritual ideal. Conversely, through the experience of faith, one's ideal comes alive. Faith is the alignment of higher truths about the soul, thinking, knowing, and willing to be a channel of blessings to others by attempting to manifest that inner pattern of perfection. As one focuses the will in this direction, an awareness of faith is the natural outcome. On the other hand, if one allows a wandering of attention to stray them from a spiritual motivation, a lack of faithfulness can appear to be the result. Faith is the substance of spirit appearing in one's conscious awareness.

Through faith, all things are possible. In the Bible we read that even faith the size of a mustard seed can accomplish the seemingly impossible. This suggests that any time we are the least bit in alignment with our divine nature and are willing to be used as a channel of activity, the spirit can move mountains. By striving to apply cooperation, by using the knowledge we have gained in coming to know ourselves, by choosing a spiritual motivation, and by cultivating our faith, the activities of spirit become a living thing in our experience. This is not an intellectual exercise. It is an active awareness that brings to our consciousness the truth about our relationship with the Divine. Faith is the direct awareness and experience of the unseen. Faith is a growing thing. It is developed by the use of it.

EXPERIENCING FAITH IN GOD,
FAITH IN OTHERS,
AND FAITH IN OURSELVES

Ultimately, our development is in direct proportion to the amount of faith we allow into our lives. Although we might not label it as such, faith is demonstrated by right-action and right-thought. To the same degree that we attempt to manifest the Christ Consciousness—the soul's inner pattern of perfection—the presence of faith is brought to conscious awareness. As we begin doing all that we know to do, the next step, the next action, the next act of service is shown to us. Our faith is cultivated as we seek to be a channel of the Creator's activity in the earth:

> Let the shadow pass. Look to the hope that springs anew, that has prompted thee to arise and go to them in His name. Be thou strong in the might of thy Lord. Be thou ready not as sacrifice, but as He has given, His pleasure rather is in service unto thy fellow man. Thus may the paths be made straight. Thus may those toils, those troubles, those conditions that have upset thee mentally, bring again the pure flowing spiritual aid into thy soul, thy body, thy mind. Keep those things near and dear. Let those sentiments that are often called of the mind grow deeper, for a *purpose*—that thou mayest fulfill thy purpose in Him. Let Him have His way. Let Him guide thee. Keep the faith—keep the faith—keep the faith! 378-26

Too often we may separate the experience of faith into: faith in God, faith in others, and faith in ourselves. We may stumble and forget to exercise our faith in God. On occasions it is our faith in other people that appears to be lacking. Sometimes, we momentarily lose faith in ourselves. And yet, this very separation suggests that faith is the belief in a thing rather than an awareness to be experienced. Beliefs can change and even cease to be of relevance, but true faith can only be lived:

> In the abilities, keep in the way in which ye judge not, if ye would not be judged. Remember, with what measure ye mete to others must eventually be meted to thee. If ye would have friends, if ye would have love, if ye would have patience, manifest same. Each of these are the attributes of the spirit of truth and as ye apply same in thy experience, the greater becomes thy measure of faith. For if ye have not faith in others, how can ye have faith in God? If ye have not faith in God, how can ye find it in thyself? 5079-1

The readings suggest that our faith in God is strengthened by right-thought and right-action as well as by the cultivation of a personal relationship with Him. From Cayce's perspective, God is not some impersonal force but rather a caring Parent who is desirous of being in partnership with us:

> To have faith in God one must know of Him and talk with Him often. One must walk with Him in the night, yea in the light, yea in all manner of places. Remember, His hand may guide thee. 3234-1

It is easy to forget that God is mindful of everything about us. Faith is strengthened as we realize that, as individuals, we are incapable of meeting every situation in our lives unaided. In the Scriptures we read:

> Therefore I say unto you, Take no thought for

your life, what ye shall eat, or what ye shall drink;
nor yet for your body, what ye shall put on. Is not
the life more than meat, and the body more than
raiment? Behold the fowls of the air: for they sow
not, neither do they reap, nor gather into barns; yet
your heavenly Father feedeth them. Are ye not
much better than they . . . Therefore take no thought,
saying, What shall we eat? or, What shall we drink?
or, Wherewithal shall we be clothed? . . . for your
heavenly Father knoweth that ye have need of all
these things. But seek ye first the kingdom of God,
and his righteousness; and all things shall be added
unto you.
                                          Matthew 6:25-26, 31-33

This does not mean for us to sit idly and wait for the
things of the physical world to come to us—for even the
birds of the air must seek out the food that the Creator
has provided for them—rather it suggests that aspects of
our mental and spiritual lives need to take precedence
over the "things" of the earth. Our divine privilege is to
cultivate the seeds of faith and to begin to see the results
that will spring forth from our efforts—physically, mentally, and spiritually:

Do not lose faith in *self,* for if faith is lost in self
and self's abilities to accomplish, then there is already defeat staring thee in the face! This would be
true for every individual. Becoming discouraged
only lessens the capacities of individuals to become
aware of that consciousness of the divine forces and
divine rights that may be sought by each individual . . . 257-131

Daily, we are reflections of our faith. All manner of
things may be accomplished when we lay aside every

fear and reach for that He would have us do. The Edgar Cayce material encourages us to open ourselves as channels of God's love in the earth and have complete faith that He will abide with us. Let us keep to that faith which is worthy of the wholeness we possess. If we would be His children, He would be our God.

CONCLUSION

The awareness of one's faith expands through any activity which opens our hearts and our minds to that divine essence—thought, service, prayer, or meditation. True faith needs to become an active, living part of every moment of our lives. We cannot speak one way to the Divine in the silence of meditation, and yet another to our neighbor in the light of day. We cannot think ourselves of little worth and then expect the Creative Forces to flow through us. Faith implies an awareness of our heritage. We are co-workers with God. We possess a pattern of wholeness that may be sparked into consciousness by our own motivation. Our destiny is to begin fulfilling all that we know to do. Our life's experiences, its joys, its sorrows, the awareness that comes to us, are all in direct proportion to the faith we exercise.

Faith is an awareness longing to be expressed. It is a birthright that may develop and grow as we do, becoming a greater part of our consciousness. It undergirds the direction of our lives, creating a vehicle through which the Divine can enter into the earth. It is an inner sense of the soul's relationship with the Creator. It is an open acknowledgment, a living-trust, in the evidence of things not seen:

Yet we know, or find, that the kingdom of heaven is within; and that the awareness, the awakening comes from within. Then through faith, through the gift of the Son and the faith in Him, we become more and more aware of the abiding presence of the spirit—the movement—as prompted by the Father; and not of self. 262-119

Ultimately, faith is sufficient to see us through every trial. We possess the same birthright as all those who have gone before us and succeeded through the exercising of their own faith. The same mind that was in Jesus, our Elder Brother, is available for our every situation and need. The readings would have us cling to that knowledge, allowing our faith to lead us to where our Creator would have us go. Faith is the awareness made manifest that we are children of God.

And finally, according to the Cayce readings, faith is the cornerstone of virtue and understanding.

VIRTUE AND UNDERSTANDING

Finally, brethren, whatsoever things are true, whatsoever things are honest, whatsoever things are just, whatsoever things are pure, whatsoever things are lovely, whatsoever things are of good report; if there be any virtue, and if there be any praise, think on these things.   Philippians 4:8

MEDITATION AFFIRMATION

Let virtue and understanding be in me, for my defense is in Thee, O Lord, my Redeemer; for Thou hearest the prayer of the upright in heart. 262-17

VIRTUE AND UNDERSTANDING

Introduction

*God, then, brought this world into being through faith,
through virtue, through understanding. Would ye know
His ways? They are not past finding out; for there is innate in each individual that which makes for a way of
association, and of understanding, to Him . . . 539-1*

As children of God, one of our purposes for being in the
earth is to express our relationship with Him through co-
creating our lives, our experiences, and our interactions
with others. The level of this co-creation is bounded only
by the limitations of our own application and awareness.
We are a part of God's laws, not simply observers of
them. As an analogy, in the physical world there are high-
way rules and speed limits that are in effect even if a
driver has overlooked the traffic signs. In the same manner, we are subject to spiritual laws which govern our
lives even if we choose to remain unaware of what they
might be.

An understanding of spiritual laws comes through experience and through attempting to live more in accord
with the Creator's will. With such understanding comes
a deep awareness of who we truly are, and a more sincere personal relationship with ourselves, with our Creator, and with all others. Both faith and virtue originate
at the soul level. Whereas, faith is an inner awareness,
virtue is a soul quality that we can manifest in our daily
lives. In this respect, virtue is anything that is good, anything that is in line with the fruits of the spirit (for example, love, justice, mercy, peace, kindness, etc.).

Cayce's approach to spiritual transformation inextricably links virtue with understanding. From the readings

perspective, virtue is essentially an innate spiritual quality; whereas true understanding comes with the application of that very same quality. Virtue is a response that originates at the soul level. It is a portion of wholeness and purity that already exists within us. Virtue is our attunement to the will of the Creative Forces; therefore, any virtue connects us with God. True understanding is the experience of the Creator's laws in the earth. True understanding is beyond reason, for it is a *knowing* that has been applied. To the same degree we attempt to exemplify virtues in our life, our understanding will grow:

> Virtue, in this study, then, is to be as the criterion with which thine faith is to be put into active service; for without that pureness of the virtue of self's own mental, material and spiritual self, there can come little understanding . . . In the application of that as has been gained comes the understanding. Be true to that that is pure in thy purpose, for *this is* virtue. In virtue comes understanding; for they are as the tenon and the mortise, they fit one with, one to, another. 262-18

Where there is virtue there will be understanding, for virtue cannot exist without it. Understanding is the pathway through which virtue is applied in daily life. Virtue and understanding are expressions of the activities of soul forces manifesting through us. When virtue becomes the basis for our thought-processes, our personal path to true understanding is made clear. Therefore, as we apply the fruits of the spirit, our perception changes so that we understand the purposefulness of all that we encounter.

Virtue is living up to the very best that we know. It is a pureness of heart, a pureness of mind, and a pureness of soul. Virtue is an attribute whereby we may see God manifested in the earth through us. Virtue is being true to our inner purposes and intent. It is holding steadfast to our highest spiritual ideal. Since it is measured against personal awareness, it will be different for every individual. Virtue is full inner cooperation that allows for enlightenment within and promotes service without. It comes as a result of our faith. Virtue enables us to know ourselves as we are known by God. Our degree of virtue is limited only by our understanding, and our understanding depends upon our virtue.

KNOWLEDGE VS. UNDERSTANDING

There is quite a difference between having knowledge and possessing understanding. Knowledge is associated with information or facts. Knowledge can be obtained through education, through hearing, through reading, even through observing. However, understanding is much more. Understanding moves beyond mere facts and becomes an activity of personal experience. Understanding is a living awareness that cannot be taught. It is the dynamic that makes information of any kind practical as well as a portion of one's awareness at a soul level:

It is known and may be experienced by the entity that not mere knowledge makes for understanding, but the application of what may be given that it, the experience, becomes a portion of the entity, of the soul, *in* application, makes for the growth. For the knowledge of the Creative Forces, the knowledge of God, is a growth. For ye grow in grace, in knowledge, in understanding, in the application of that thou hast experienced and dost experience in thy relationships to thy fellow man. 884-1

In other words, it is not so much what we know (or

what we think we know) that counts in our attempt to understand our relationship with God; instead, it is what we apply—what we do about what we know—that provides for personal transformation.

Obtaining knowledge can be a step toward a true growth in understanding; however, Cayce warned against acquiring knowledge simply for the sake of having information at one's disposal. In fact, he stated that the more we know the more we are ultimately responsible for attempting to apply in our personal lives. Any knowledge not applied becomes a "sin" of omission—a shortcoming whereby we are held accountable for knowing to do something and yet not doing it. In addition, knowledge acquired and not lived does not become a part of one's awareness at the soul level.

For example, over the years countless individuals have expressed their appreciation for the readings' philosophy because it "made sense" or because it has given them the knowledge that "life is a purposeful experience." That knowledge suggests that we are constantly molding and shaping our tomorrows. That knowledge suggests that we are personally responsible for our relationship with ourselves, one another, and our God. That knowledge should move us to become more aware of our thoughts, our deeds, and our interactions with others. If it persuades us to make some positive changes in our lives, it becomes a part of the soul's awareness in future experiences. If applied, it will become something that will remain with us. On the other hand, if it only remains at the level of knowledge, it has no permanent effect upon us—it does not change our inner awareness:

With the perfect understanding of any law, the law may be made a part of the entity, and as the development through the physical plane is to gain the understanding of all universal laws, the knowledge

thus attained and made a part of the entity, brings
the development . . . Hence the necessity of the
given force as was said, "My son, in all thy getting,
get understanding," and the ability to apply same.
900-25

True understanding has such a powerful effect upon
bringing faith into conscious awareness, Cayce told the
original study group that an individual with true understanding "may move mountains." (262-19)

THE PERCEPTION OF VIRTUES CAN
LEAD TO GREATER UNDERSTANDING

Many of us spend a great deal of time and energy expressing judgment and criticism. Regardless of whether
this condemnation is directed inward or outward, it has
a far-reaching effect upon our personal perception. In
fact, each time we critique someone or something in a
negative fashion, the easier it becomes for us to see what
is "wrong" instead of what is "right," the easier it becomes for us to become judgmental. Remember, whatever we apply, positively or negatively, becomes a greater
portion of our individual awareness.

This same approach, judging other people rather than
attempting to understand that they possess the same
divine spark as do we, has long been a negative human
tendency. Cayce told a group of his supporters:

Suppose, for the moment, that God looked on
thine own heart as thou hast oft looked on thine
brother's life? *Oblivion . . .Think—think—*on these
things! 254-68

It is sobering to ponder what would happen if our Creator were to begin judging us in the same manner we

have often critiqued others. However, rather than condemning ourselves for what we have been doing wrong,
we simply need to begin changing the ways in which we
view ourselves and others. In terms of working with our
individual perceptions, the readings suggest that it is
important for us to begin "minimizing the faults and
magnifying the virtues" of everyone with whom we come
in contact:

> . . . we would minimize the faults and magnify
> the virtues. And this the entity should adopt as its
> first principle, in the changing of its life as it goes to
> seek new opportunities. Quit finding fault with oth-
> ers and others will quit finding fault with you. This
> is the first thing to adopt in thy new life. And let this
> be a new experience for you—to recognize the abili-
> ties as well as the faults. 3544-1

How often do we go out of our way (or simply take the
time) to discuss, or think, what is "right" about a person,
rather than what is "wrong" with them?

But more than just attempting to perceive the virtues
in those with whom we have previously had personality
conflicts, the readings state that we are not to condemn
anyone. This might prove more difficult in terms of dealing with those we believe have wronged us as well as
those who have wronged another person. And yet, regardless of what an individual has done, he or she is still
a child of God. The Bible states "judge not lest ye be
judged" (Matthew 7:1). Because we may never know the
trials or challenges an individual has faced, we have no
justification in exercising condemnation. Only if we had
personally experienced an individual's life path could we
even hope to understand what led to certain behavior.
Virtue does not suggest that we condone negative or
even criminal behavior, but it does suggest we cannot

hold grudges or personally condemn. Good can be found and cultivated in everyone, we just need to know how to look for it.

Since virtue is associated with purity, it sees past all criticism and condemnation. Depending upon the circumstance, this might be as simple as attempting to see the positive that others can see, or perhaps it is simply not contributing to the gossip we might hear about another person. Even if we are not always successful, the readings suggest that each time we *try* to do what is right, it has a positive effect upon our growing awareness and understanding.

WHOLENESS AS AN
ACTIVITY OF THE SPIRIT

Our inner wholeness is quickened and unfolded through virtue and understanding. The key to discovering that wholeness is by awakening to our spiritual essence within. Much of nature follows this very same principle. For example, the beauty of the rose grows from within (to be sure, absorbing those things from the environment without), but its pattern, its model for wholeness, resides deep within the seed of itself. This is also true for each one of us. By attempting to live in accord with the fruits of the spirit, we awaken to our own divine nature. Within each of us there is a desire for wholeness. We possess the pattern, even the desire to become all that we can be. This goal is not reached by a single leap, but rather step by step, a little at a time:

Well that this be understood, that virtue and understanding deals primarily with self and self's relationship to the Creative Forces, or God, and that virtue and understanding in self is *reflected* in self, rather than a *judgment* upon another. Judge self by thine understanding and thine own virtue, *not* another—for these are of the spirit and must be judged by the spirit. "Judge not that ye be not judged." 262-19

Virtue and understanding are the link between ourselves and the Creative Forces. Through virtue and understanding, God's laws of spirituality may be activated in the physical world. The more we desire and attempt to be channels of His love and blessings to others, the more we may feel His all-abiding presence, the more His power may flow through us unto others. When our Elder Brother, Jesus, fed five thousand individuals with only five loaves and two fishes, it was a clear indication that he possessed a true understanding of God's laws. In fact, His understanding was so complete that even the consciousness of the five thousand was lifted, and they were supplied with their need. To some this would appear miraculous, for it would seem to defy rational understanding. Yet, in the truest sense, a miracle is only the lawful unfoldment of God's laws.

Virtue and understanding are required for any spiritual activity. Virtue and understanding undergird our lives with a spiritual power that shapes and molds our awareness of all that we see, all that we do, and all that we have drawn to us. Virtue possesses the spiritual lawfulness of God manifesting in the earth. It strengthens our knowledge of the Creator and facilitates even greater faith in Him. Understanding is a path which never wavers for its intent and purpose is grounded in universal laws and the love of God. Together, virtue and understanding form the foundation of a new way of life—an approach that recognizes we are spiritual beings in the earth, not simply mental and physical creatures.

DO WHAT YOU KNOW TO DO

There will always be occasions in life when we desire to look up and reach for something higher, regardless of what accomplishments we achieve or how low we may feel at any given moment. Because our natural state is spiritual, we possess a longing for experiencing a closer walk with God. This closeness will come as a result of doing His will—of seeking to be His companions in the earth. It is a desire for this closeness with our spiritual source that leads us to virtue and understanding. In fact, our path becomes clearer as we cultivate the singleness of purpose to do His work.

The power of the Creator can awaken within each one of us the remembrance of our heritage as His children. Our inner self longs for that consciousness that comes with abiding in Him. Within itself, the soul finds its true relationship with its Creator. This inner pattern for wholeness is awakened by our spiritual motivation:

> It is not how much one knows that counts, but how well one applies that it knows; in just being, doing, thinking, that which is pointed out to self through such constant, consistent, *practical* dependence upon the Creative Forces that have promised ever to meet one—every one—when sought. And there will come that which is for the greater development in the soul forces of such an one that seeks. 270-33

One frequently mentioned motto in the Cayce reading is to "do what you know to do and the next step will be given." Too often the distance between where we are and where we want to go seems overwhelming. And yet, the readings advise us to take one step at a time, line upon line, precept upon precept, here a little there a little.

Knowing to do good and not doing it is perhaps the greatest error we can make, for it is only by doing what we know to do that our next step is made clear. By simply choosing aright, by simply doing the best we find within ourselves, we will be guided by a pattern of wholeness—our own spiritual source. Only in such a manner may we meet the daily challenges of life and avoid straying from our proper destiny.

CONCLUSION

Virtue is the very best we have inside of us. It is a fruit of the spirit. It is a portion of our true self. Our virtues reveal our true potential for they are innate, simply waiting to be awakened and expressed. Understanding becomes ours as we move beyond the knowledge of facts and begin living that knowledge until it becomes a personal expression of our true selves. Virtue and understanding is moral excellence applied. Virtue and understanding allow for the awareness that He is our pattern and would work through us if we would allow Him. We must be both persistent and consistent in our activities. As we put into practice the things of the spirit, love, kindness, forgiveness, and patience, we transform ourselves and positively affect the world around us:

For it is not what one knows that counts but rather what one does about that one knows! For it is line upon line, precept upon precept, here a little, there a little. For ye grow in grace and in knowledge and in understanding as ye apply that in thine experience that makes the paths straight, that keeps upon the way that is constructive in the experience. 954-4

Keeping ourselves unspotted from the world, condemning no one, leaving behind those things which are out of harmony with His spiritual lawfulness, and turning our face to the Light—in this manner we will find ourselves on the pathway of virtue and understanding. We will find love in ourselves, in one another, and in our Creator—no one will be beyond these bounds. We will find the earth not as a place of trials and challenges and of desires to be fulfilled, but as a place of His loving service. We will be renewed in our efforts to move forward, giving thanks for our understanding from within: the fact that each of us is a part of the Whole.

With the proper motivation, all the good we ever accomplish is built within the fiber of our being. It is by our selfless deeds and thoughts, that we gradually rise in consciousness. We will recognize we are on the path of virtue and understanding whenever we have no unkind thoughts of another. We will recognize we are on this path when we begin to see ourselves as our Creator sees us:

So live then each day that some portion may add to thy inner, thy better, thy soul self. Thus may ye gain strength, ye may gain knowledge—and virtue; in such measures that life with its experiences becomes more and more worthwhile, with more joy. 1745-1

LESSON SIX

FELLOWSHIP

. . . I will put my law in their inward parts, and write it in their hearts; and I will be their God, and they shall be my people. Jeremiah 31:33

MEDITATION AFFIRMATION

How excellent is Thy name in the earth, O Lord! Would I have fellowship with Thee, I must show brotherly love to my fellow man. Though I come in humbleness and have aught against my brother, my prayer, my meditation, does not rise to Thee. Help Thou my efforts in my approach to Thee. 262-21

FELLOWSHIP

Introduction

Doing unto others as ye would have them do unto you is the extreme test of fellowship. Without same ye may not wholly please God. 262-22

Let that rather be thy watchword, "I am my brother's keeper." Who is thy brother? Whoever, wherever he is, that bears the imprint of the Maker in the earth, be he black, white, gray or grizzled, be he young, be he Hottentot, or on the throne or in the president's chair. All that are in the earth today are thy brothers. 2780-3

The Edgar Cayce material assures us that from the beginning of time we have had a relationship with God, although that knowledge is no longer at the conscious level. Part of our heritage is to experience this relationship in full awareness and with an understanding of our connectedness with one another. An extremely important (and sometimes challenging) aspect of personal transformation is to begin to become aware of the joint fellowship we all possess. We share a common bond—a spiritual community with all other individuals. Since He is our Creator, we are all part of the same Whole, and deep within ourselves we each have this awareness. From the readings' perspective, this spiritual connection desires to be made manifest in the earth.

At the very core of each individual is the consciousness of a seeker. Each of us possesses a longing for the realization of fellowship or spiritual community. Within each of us there is a pattern of wholeness which continually moves us in search of fulfillment, service, and love for one another. By becoming attuned to this inner pattern, we gain the realization of true fellowship. This inner spark propels us toward the fullest possible relationship with our Creator. Too often, in our limited understanding of this spiritual desire, we attempt to satisfy this craving with material pursuits and every manner of possible escape. But escape can only lead to feelings of even greater emptiness, for this soul longing can only be satisfied with the things of the spirit: selflessness, service, and love.

Fellowship is the realization of our connection with one another and our joint connection with God. As we become more conscious of this relationship, we become more aware of our obligation to all individuals within the world community. We awaken within ourselves to the realization that He is a part of others in the same way that He is a part of us. As we allow the Creator's love to flow through us, we come to the understanding that the kinship we share with one another as human beings is but a faint reflection of an even deeper spiritual connection. Through fellowship, we become aware of our oneness with all of God's children.

OUR RESPONSIBILITY
TO ONE ANOTHER

Edgar Cayce believed that a day would arrive in the history of the world when humankind finally realized its responsibility to each individual. In response to the biblical question, "Am I my brother's keeper?" the answer was a resounding YES! The world is but one community of which we are all a part. Though a "sister" or a "brother" may be on the other side of the world (or right next door) we are responsible for all that we find to do in relationship to them.

From a practical standpoint, what part can we play in the fulfillment of this divine plan? Each of us is provided with tasks and opportunities that come into our lives as a means of helping someone else. In whatever realm we find ourselves, there is still the chance to provide some small act of service. To be of service does not mean to perform some wondrous deed, or to necessarily touch the lives of thousands. The pattern set by our Elder Brother, Jesus, was to assist one individual at a time, just as they presented themselves. Our personal opportunities to be of assistance already exist within our own grasp. The ways in which we treat others through patience, through kindness, through compassion and love, might be the very act of service we are being called to do. To simply help someone help themselves might be the greatest service of all. Whatever small thing we find to do is often the very deed the Creator has placed in our path as a means of being a channel of His love:

And unless each soul entity (and this entity especially) makes the world better, that corner or place of the world a little better, a little bit more hopeful, a little bit more patient, showing a little more of brotherly love, a little more of kindness, a little more of long-suffering—by the very words and deeds of the entity, the life is a failure; especially so far as growth is concerned. Though you gain the whole world, how little ye must think of thyself if ye lose the purpose for which the soul entered this particular sojourn! Think not more highly of thyself than ye ought to think, yet no one will think more of you than you do of yourself; not in egotism, but in the desire to be of a help. For who is the greatest? He that is the servant of all, he that contributes that which makes each soul glad to be alive, glad to have the opportunity to contribute something to the welfare of his brother. 3420-1

The divine within seeks to be a channel of service in the material world. Our God has compassion for each one of us, just as a parent has unconditional love for a child. It is through us that His assistance might be made manifest in the earth. When we fail to provide another with forgiveness, or compassion, or some small act of kindness, we fail in our responsibility to the earth—to the community that binds us together. We fail to live up to our responsibility as His children. Cayce suggested that as long as we are alive, we have the opportunity to be of assistance to someone else.

Ours is the opportunity to begin seeing a spark of good in everyone. As we begin to minimize an individual's faults and magnify his or her virtues, we come to the realization that what can change most in our interactions with others is our own perception—for even our own worst "enemy" has a best friend. This does not mean that we need to accept blindly all that another person does or stands for, rather we are challenged to begin seeing others in the same way that the Creator sees them (and us). By so doing, we come to the awareness that everyone is worthy of our love, our kindness, our compassion, our guidance, even our service:

> For ye have not begun to think straight until ye are able to see in the life of those whom ye utterly dislike, something ye would worship in thy Maker. For each soul-entity in the earth, with life, whether of this, or that shade or color, or whether this or that disfigurement of body or mind, is in the earth by the grace of God. For He has not willed that any soul should perish, and has thus prepared a way of escape. And ye, as His servant, as the child of the living God, are given the opportunity to contribute to the welfare of any whom ye even consider not quite on par with thy opportunity. Thus if ye belittle oth-

ers, what sort of a tree will grow in thine own heart?
Ye may be sure someone else will belittle thee.
3575-2

In addition, as we see the good in others, we have the
opportunity to assist them in recognizing the strengths
they have to offer and magnify them in the process.

We must come to love our neighbor (regardless of how
vast the distances between us) just as our Creator loves
us. Each individual of every land, of every color, of every
creed, is a part of us—each contributes to the Whole. We
are all members of the same community. We are all por-
tions of God.

> Q. Please describe the difference in fellowship and
> brotherhood.
> A. One to God, the other to man. 262-22

And it is only as ye deal with thy fellow man that
ye show forth His love. For as ye do it unto the least
of these, thy brethren, ye do it unto thy Maker
1620-1

OUR RELATIONSHIP WITH GOD

What could be more beautiful than the entire earth
being one community under God? In spite of the fact
that this may seem impossible or even far from the
present reality, the readings confirm the fact that this is
the destiny of humankind. This question regarding the
world appearing so divided and yet sharing a joint destiny prompted one of the members of the original study
group to ask, "Can brotherhood exist among men without true fellowship?" Cayce responded:

Fellowship is first brotherhood, a pattern of—or

a shadow of—what fellowship is; for, as has been given, all one sees manifest in a material world is but a reflection or a shadow of the real or the spiritual life. Brotherhood, then, is an expression of the fellowship that exists in the *spiritual* life. 262-23

What the readings are suggesting is the fact that this unity, this oneness under God already exists at the spiritual level. Our challenge is to somehow bring that awareness into consciousness in the material world. We can begin today. Regardless of what place we find ourselves right now, the opportunity is ours to manifest love, to share fellowship, and to evoke community in our home, at work, and in our daily surroundings. The readings state that from our limited perspective, we cannot begin to imagine the effect this will have upon the people around us. We cannot begin to conceive of the change this will have upon our own hearts. We cannot possibly fathom the good this will have upon the earth:

Remember then as this: There are promises made by the Creative Forces or God to the children of men, that "If ye will be my daughter, my son, my child, I will indeed be thy God." This is an individual promise. Hence the purposes are for an entrance that the *soul* may be prepared for an indwelling with the soul, the mind of a living God. 1436-1

The more we respond to one another in a spirit of community and brotherhood, the greater will be the Creator's capacity to work through us as His children abiding in the earth.

Throughout every generation, our greatest need as individuals has been to understand our true relationship with one another and with our Creator. We might ask, "What does our relationship with one another have to do with our relationship with God?" In the ultimate sense, it is impossible to come to know one without the other, for God is inseparable from His creations. All souls were made in His likeness. We are not simply physical bodies, but are rather souls who find ourselves in the material world. In the Scriptures we read, "Inasmuch as ye have done it unto one of the least of my brethren, ye have done it unto me." (Matthew 25:40) In response to a question regarding how an individual might serve and be in greater attunement with God, the readings framed the answer in terms of the individual's personal relationships and daily interactions with others. As far as achieving a closer connection with God, the questioner was told:

> That is a natural heritage of each soul. Then, the practice of same, the application of same in the daily dealings, in the daily relationships—these bring within themselves that consciousness and that attunement wherein there may be the greater awareness . . . This, as we have indicated, is to be achieved day by day, here a little, there a little, line upon line, precept upon precept. Not as rote, but rather as a *living* experience that becomes so much the portion of self that it is felt, seen, known by all who may *meet* the body in its daily activities! A kind word, a gentle speech, even under the most trying circumstance, creates not only for self that attunement but makes same for others—or makes others aware of same. This may be illustrated to the conscious mind by how the radio may be changed high or low; or to the perfect accord, and thus bring a unison that makes for not only perfect reception but perfect reaction upon those *affected* by same. 877-6

Using Cayce's analogy, for the same reason that a radio must be attuned to the proper frequency in order to have optimal reception, it is impossible to truly love God and still continue to harbor contempt for one of His creations. Love and hate cannot reside within the same heart.

Each of us has the opportunity to be a part of the spiritual transformation of the earth—though our involvement is limited by the extent to which we are willing to become transformed. When we take time to examine how we have interacted with others, we may realize how frequently we have fallen short of our goal. Only by becoming conscious of the divine spirit within will we begin to see the world, ourselves, and others as each is seen by God. The readings frequently suggested prayer and meditation as essential for gaining this awareness of the Divine. As we seek to attune to our Creator, the harmony of His presence will fill our lives and reach out to all those we touch. Our fellowship with God develops as we reach out to those around us.

How well do we really want to know our God? From Cayce's perspective, the answer is only as much as we attempt to reach out to others.

COMMUNITY AS A RESPONSIBILITY

Too often in the day-to-day clamor and activity of our lives we forget to focus on the importance of community. Many people have found that they often forget to take the time to listen, to smile, to simply experience the presence of another person rather than moving on to the next goal they hope to achieve that day. Because of our relationship with God, we have a responsibility to all others. Not simply a duty to those who love us and whom we love in return, but there is a duty we share with everyone. The readings remind us that the Creator has par-

doned our own shortcomings and reached out with unconditional love. We are expected to do the same. The
more we gain a true awareness of our obligations to one
another, to our God, to ourselves, the greater becomes
our own capacity to reach out in the spirit of community.

To many of us this may seem difficult, even beyond
our present capabilities. And yet, would we but take God
at His promises, the way would be shown to us. Whenever we feel out of harmony with one another or with
God, it is we who have moved. He will never ask us to
accomplish more than we are able:

In consideration of fellowship, this should mean
a great deal to each and every member of this or
such a group; for with the application in their own
experience there may be expected, and there may
be received, that true fellowship in the experience
of the individual; and when such is *not* one's experience, then such ones may know they are lacking
in *their* efforts in being what they should in their
relationships to themselves, their Maker, the group.
Then, make for that which is sincere in purpose,
pure in mind, reasonable even to self, walking in the
way that brings a more close union with Him, that
"Will ye be my people, I will be your God." He seeks
to find that expression even in all who are called in
the *I am that I am,* and is an ever active force that
through all ages, all peoples, may be a memorial
that one has fellowship with Him, that brought the
Pleiades into being, that set the bands of Orion, or
the waters in the deep that are cast upon the land,
or brings breath into the life of all creatures, and
supplies the union with those creative forces that
makes for the *songs* of the spheres—the Lord is His
name! 262-23

Realizing that the innermost part of us is whole, and that the Creator of all things has ordained our ultimate success, how can we continue to believe that true fellowship is beyond the capacity of humankind? The Creator's love is destined to be made manifest in the earth, so when will we choose to do our part?

Those who would share the community of God have a duty. Those who would know His fellowship have an obligation. Unless each of us makes the world a little better, a little more hopeful, a little more patient, a little more kind, a little more loving—through our thoughts, words, and deeds—then we have not even begun to be successful in sharing with others the heritage of our spiritual fellowship. The task could be no clearer. Fellowship and brotherhood instilled into the hearts and souls of each individual will bring the world to a new millennium. But peace on earth and good will toward all must be a personal experience before it can be realized by the world. Are we doing our part to bring about this transformation?

CONCLUSION

Fellowship has yet to be manifested in our lives because we have forgotten the purpose for which we were created: to become companions and co-creators with God, to be channels of His love in the earth, and to be of service to all we find in need. Is it any wonder we often feel despondent and wander aimlessly when we have overlooked the very reason that we are here? As children of God, we have the opportunity to gain the complete awareness of our relationship with Him. But, ultimately, this awareness grows and develops only through our interactions with others—because it is through our activities with others that we demonstrate how well we have come to know our God.

Cayce frequently told individuals that until they were able to perceive a spark of the Creator within even those they disliked, they had not yet begun to think right. This "right thought" is a part of the pattern of wholeness which exists upon the fiber of one's inner self. When individuals were confused by relationships in which they had found difficulty, they were reminded that Jesus had manifested an example for all:

> Yet there is oft within the entity's own consciousness that wonderment as to whether correct choices have been made in dealing with others. At such times, then, look deep into the life of the man Jesus and see how He dealt with the problems of the day. As He gave, in the interpretation of His purpose in the earth, He recognized the needs of each soul as to its purpose in the earth also. For, all men (and He was a man) have fallen short of the glory of God. Only in Him, through Him, by Him may one attain to that true sonship, that true fellowship, that true relationship to the Creative Forces or God. 3357-2

True fellowship realizes our ultimate connection with one another and our joint connection with God.

The world yearns for the love we might offer to it. With this knowledge, how can we hold on to animosity, hatred, or judgment? Regardless of how we once perceived those we called enemies, we now have the opportunity to call them friends, to see them through the eyes of love, to desire their attunement with the Creator as well as our own. As we develop step by step, here a little, there a little, we exhibit cooperation, we become better acquainted with ourselves and with those around us, the awareness of our spiritual motivation deepens, our faith is strengthened, we manifest the qualities of virtue and understanding, and more and more we become aware of our community with God and with the world. If we would experience the abiding fellowship of this true sense of community, we must rely on His great commandment, "That you love one another." For when we do, God's fellowship and community might finally become manifested in the earth.

LESSON SEVEN

PATIENCE

In your patience possess ye your souls.   Luke 21:19

MEDITATION AFFIRMATION

How gracious is Thy presence in the earth, O Lord! Be Thou the guide, that we with patience may run the race which is set before us, looking to Thee, the Author, the Giver of light. 262-24

PATIENCE

Introduction

Patience is that necessary activity of the mind, mentally, physically, and spiritually, that makes for expansion of and acquaintance with the activities of that that may be known in self, as to whether there is the proper attitude with that which is held as the ideal, as to whether the faith is in faith or by works, whether the virtue is as with understanding or is as a set rule, whether self is in possession of the ideal, and with cooperative measures activating in the experience of individuals. Hence, as we find, this lesson must be the summing up of all that has been experienced by individuals through that they have given to others, that they now must live themselves in their daily activities . . .
262-25

In a world so focused on speed, achievement, and closure, the process of patience may be a difficult lesson to grasp. In spite of the fact that patience is the "summing up" of all that has gone before, it is frequently misunderstood. Too often individuals equate patience with passiveness or submissiveness; it is neither. From the readings perspective these emotions equate to a benign acceptance rather than to the conscious activity demanded of patience:

This is not patience, for patience is not passive nor negative; it is a *constructive* influence, a positive activative force. For, if one smite thee on the one cheek, did He say withdraw? No! Rather, turn the other! Be active in thy patience; be active in thy relationships with thy fellow man! 815-2

Patience is not receptive, instead it is active.

Sometimes people believe that patience is synonymous with tolerance, but tolerance is the acceptance of things as they appear to be, whereas patience requires becoming actively aware of all impelling influences in a situation. Rather than being a passive state of mind, Cayce suggested that true patience was an activity of the body, mind, and soul focused in such a way as to allow God's love, laws, and presence to come into our lives. From this perspective, patience is the undergirding force of all spiritual activities manifesting in the earth—it is the cornerstone of all spiritual development. Through patience our spiritual motivation evolves to such an extent that it becomes our conscious response to daily life. Patience puts service into action, allowing us to become channels of blessings to others.

According to the readings, patience is the very essence of God. Although it may take an age of ages, His desire is for all of us to come to an awareness of the Light—God is the God of patience. Therefore, patience endureth unto the end. Patience gives us a sense of our own eternity. Patience is the natural expression of a portion of the divine mind within us:

> *Learn ye patience,* if ye would have an understanding, if ye would gain harmony and grace in this experience! "For in patience do ye possess your souls." It's when individuals have become impatient, and desire their own will or desire their expression or desire that they as individuals be heard, that they become less and less in that close association with the Divine—and more of that as is human and [less] of the animal becomes manifest. 1201-2

Patience allows for the awakening of the divine within. In simplest terms, patience is love in action.

THE DEVELOPMENT OF PATIENCE

The development of patience requires attunement (meditation, prayer, and introspection), consistency, and simply becoming aware of how we react to the world around us versus how we should act:

> In this application, not the great things—but being gentle, and know, even as He gave, "In patience possess ye your souls." For, patience is not as of not getting mad; not as of toleration; for tolerance and patience are as opposite as hate and brotherly love in their field of activity. For, patience is becoming aware of that which is the impelling influence in thine experience, while tolerance is as holding your tongue when you want to say something bad! Then, in the activities as related to these, these will not only aid in creating greater influence in the experience but will make for joyousness in the everyday activities of life. 451-3

Practicing patience means that we begin to overcome reactionary responses to people, to life, and to situations, and instead act toward others in ways that are in keeping with the best that we know. Patience is saying and doing not want we want, but what we ought. And the process of being patient is much more than just being nice or showing kindness. For example, tolerance is accepting people for who they are (or at least choosing not to verbalize our judgment) but patience goes a step further and suggests that we need to see something of our divine heritage in every individual we encounter:

> *Q. When we reach the development of ceasing to see faults in those we contact, is it then we can say we have patience?*

A. When we see rather Him that we worship even
in the faults of others, *then* we are at the *beginning*
of patience. 262-24

That state of consciousness resides within and may be
awakened through attunement, application, consistency, and patience.

Dozens of individuals were told in their readings that
an essential purpose of their *entire lifetime* was to learn
the lesson of patience. Other individuals were told that a
frustrating health condition could also be seen as an
opportunity for them to learn patience. In response to
one individual's desire to see immediate results, Cayce
stated:

Give the *time!* Be *patient!* You've had years and
years of the disturbance. Don't expect it to be cured
in a moment and be of a permanent nature. For the
body, the life, the whole of every entity *is* a *growth;*
and unless it is of such a growth that it is stable, it
isn't worth very much! Be patient. Be consistent. Be
persistent. 716-3

Instead of seeing patience as an ongoing lesson of
growth and development, most of us have been condi-
tioned to want to have results immediately: *I want to
learn patience and I want to learn it NOW!* Results, however, may not be seen so quickly. An analogy used by
Cayce was that an individual does not sow a seed and
then constantly dig it up to see what has happened. It
takes time, faith, and persistency. However, patience
should not be confused with waiting:

Do not just sit still and wait! Do something about
self and self's abilities to make for greater mental
and physical reactions, about those things that are

to be met in the experience of this body, [529], at this time! 529-1

Then we would define for the entity what we mean by the entity having patience—in an active, positive manner and not merely as a passive thing. Taking or enduring hardships, or censure, or idiosyncrasies of others, is not necessarily patience at all. It may become merely that of being a drudge not only to self but an outlet of expression from others that may never be quite satisfying because there is no resistance. Passive patience, to be sure, has its place; but consider patience rather from the precepts of God's relationship to man: love unbounded is patience. Love manifested is patience. Endurance at times is patience, consistence ever is patience. 3161-1

Patience is developed whenever we consistently and persistently attempt to manifest God's activity in the earth. In other words, whenever we attempt to reach out in wholeness through service, love, compassion, or even healing. Patience is purposeful action grounded in spiritual motivation.

Because patience undergirds the realization of spiritual development, it must become an active, growing force which rises up to meet every situation in our lives. Patience sees every experience as a personal opportunity for growth. Patience understands every challenge as the chance to demonstrate that we have gained an awareness of His laws in the earth. How will we know when our patience is fully developed? When we recognize God in everyone, and when our every act, our every thought, our every word, and our every deed is established in Him. True patience fills us with the peace of His all-abiding presence.

PATIENCE WITH SELF AND OTHERS

Patience with self implies we have become conscious of the fact that we have more to learn. Each of us is intimately aware of our internal thoughts and response patterns toward ourselves and others. Through the application of patience, our responses can become more in keeping with the best we have within ourselves. In fact, until our thoughts and deeds are in alignment with the Christ pattern within, the lesson of patience has not yet been realized. When we are patient with ourselves, we do not become frustrated or self-condemning when we have yet to achieve our goal. Instead, we encourage ourselves with perseverance and determination to continue trying. The readings often stated that we were responsible for the "try"—doing the best that we knew to do; God was responsible for the results:

These be the things one must do. And do find patience with self. It has been said, "Have we not piped all the day long and no one has answered?" Seekest thou, as was given from this illustration, for the gratifying of thy self? or seekest thou to be a channel of blessing to thy fellow man? They may not have answered as *thou* hast seen. They may have even shown contempt, as sneering, for thy patience and thy trouble. But *somewhere* the sun still shines; *somewhere* the day is done; for those that have grown weary, for those that have given up. The Lord abhorreth the quitter. And those temptations that come in such cases are the viewing of thine own *self.* Ye have hurt thyself and ye have again crucified thy Lord, when ye become impatient or speak harshly because someone has jeered or because someone has sneered or because someone has laughed at thy efforts! Leave the *results,* leave the

giving of the crown, leave the glory, with the Lord!
He will repay! Thou sayest in thine own heart that
thou believest. Then merely, simply, *act* that way! In
speech, in thought, in deed. 518-2

Ultimately, the only person we can change is ourselves. We cannot force others to interact with us in a
manner we desire. However, we can consistently respond to them in the same manner we would like to be
treated in return.

Within the dynamic of all human relationships is the
undergirding principle of "like attracts like." We must
develop within ourselves what we would hope to receive
from another. In other words, as we put out the best that
we know, we cannot help but draw back toward us the
same thing in return:

The more patience that is shown in self toward
others, the more patience will be shown by others
to self—and it becomes then a circle, as it were, and
before one knows it the conditions have adjusted
themselves so that the self is able to adapt self to all
the circumstances and conditions, and the environs that come about in the various activities. Being patient, then, with self first, being patient then
with others. As the patience is manifest, so will the
results be seen. This doesn't mean patience in the
sense of just submissiveness, or just being quiet—
but an *active* patience, *conscious* of being patient
with self and with others. Force self to do some un-
pleasant things that it hasn't wanted to do once in a
while, and like it! 911-3

Interestingly enough, the readings contend that when
we believe our patience has completely worn out with another person we have actually lost patience with ourselves.

It is easy to become so caught up in our daily activities that we forget the reason for which we were given life in the first place—Cayce called it running the race of life. Day by day, moment by moment, we have an opportunity to be a channel of God's activities to those around us. Our challenge is to carry the virtue of patience with us at all times, becoming conscious of the fact that our every life experience has the capacity to bring us into closer attunement with Him. We are being called upon to lay aside those things that would hinder us and to accomplish instead the very best that we know. This is the way to wholeness. Patiently, the Creator waits upon our success.

PATIENCE AS A STATE OF AWARENESS

Most of us have experienced problems which were so challenging that we questioned our ability to cope. On other occasions, difficulties that others might have found insurmountable were handled as if we had solved them before. The readings suggest that there is a difference between having knowledge and possessing a true state of awareness. Having knowledge suggests that one knows something and can use or disregard the information; possessing an awareness implies that something has become a part of an individual's very state of being. Lessons learned through patience become a part of our soul which remains for all eternity. In fact, a lesson learned through patience becomes a part of our consciousness to such an extent that we might find ourselves an example to others. We are challenged to constantly apply and work with patience, but until it becomes a state of awareness—our true and natural response—we have not learned it:

Would we have that love, that patience of the
Maker of the worlds, we must show patience to our
brother, and—as was asked of Him, how oft shall I
forgive? Seven times? Yea, seventy times seven, that
ye may know that which is builded in self. Through
patience does the understanding come. Knowledge
of itself is nothing. Understanding in the Lord becomes that of love, in patience, that maketh for the
glorifying of that which is the gift of the Father in
the material, the mental, the spiritual world. Stand
still, will ye see the glory of the Lord. In patience
possess ye your souls. As there is gained more and
more those understandings in cooperation, self,
activities in self, and the more there is gained a
knowledge of the presence of Him in the experience, greater does patience work in the life, the
experience, the heart, and the soul grows in understanding of His presence . . . 262-24

Patience truly exercised brings a greater awareness,
for it tests the boundaries of our development. To the
extent we possess patience, we come to understand what
we have done with our knowledge. Through patience we
can begin to see life's challenges as opportunities for
growth. Through patience we come to understand our
relationship with the Creator, as well as His relationship
with us. With patience we are enabled to manifest the
virtues of the spirit, for in patience we possess our souls.

PATIENCE AS A DIMENSION

Edgar Cayce stated that our awareness of the world
was bounded by three dimensions. Although seemingly
matter-of-fact, what may have surprised his listeners
was the assertion that those dimensions were time,
space, and patience! From Cayce's perspective, time and

space allowed individuals to see the results of their previous thoughts and actions, while patience provided for
the awareness of the continuity of life and the eternality
of the soul. The three dimensions were created as a
means of humankind coming to understand their true
identity as well as their relationship with God:

> Thus we find His intervention in man's attempt
> throughout the eons of time and space. For these
> (time and space) become portions of this three-di-
> mensional plane. And what is the other? Time,
> Space, Patience! For God has shown and does show
> us day by day, even as His Son gave, that in patience
> we become aware of our souls, of our identity, of our
> being each a corpuscle, as it were, in the great body,
> in the heart of, our God. 262-114

The readings suggested that patience, just like time
and space, was without beginning or end. Even more
challenging to human comprehension is the statement
that, in truth, *there is only patience* and that time and
space are simply tools for understanding and growth
which do not exist beyond the confines of the earth:

> Time and space and patience are most needed
> oft, that few souls or individuals are willing to pay
> the price for—until they grow to be such, you see.
> Just as has so oft been indicated, one doesn't fall out
> of a tree into heaven, or an airplane, or fly into
> heaven, but one grows in grace, in knowledge, in
> understanding, in perfecting within self those ap-
> plications of tenets and truths that bring to the ac-
> tivities the spiritual, the mental growth. 2746-2

> Then there is no time, there is no space, when
> patience becomes manifested in love. 3161-1

Frequently, individuals were reminded of the biblical statement "In patience possess ye your souls." When this is approached from the perspective of patience as a dimension—the dimension of all that there is—it suggests that our growing consciousness will eventually lead to the awareness that there is only one force undergirding the activity of the universe. In spite of our current (and limited) human perspective, ultimately God is all that exists.

CONCLUSION

Each of us is in the process of development whereby we can come to understand our true relationship with God. We are His spiritual children, finding that knowledge of ourselves in the physical world. Patience is the bridge connecting who we are with who we will ultimately become:

> Be *glad* you have the opportunity to be alive at this time, and to be a part of that preparation for the coming influences of a spiritual nature that *must* rule the world. These are indicated, and these are part of thy experience. Be happy of it, and give thanks daily for it. 2376-3

Patience is an indication of our own development. With it we can meet every weakness within ourselves and begin to make way for the very best that we have to offer. Patience provides us with deeper insights into life, a clearer vision of what we can be about, and a broader understanding of our true relationship with ourselves and with one another. As we develop in our awareness of what it means to be a channel of blessings, we are better able to allow God's love, laws, even His presence, to become manifested in the earth through us. As we seek to awaken our inner selves, becoming more attuned to our inner pattern of wholeness—the Christ Consciousness—we begin to realize that our life experience is drawn to us only as a means of becoming aware of ourselves and of discovering where we are out of alignment with our own journey toward wholeness.

Because God has been so patient with each of us, we should find it within ourselves to be patient with one another. When we show a lack of patience or self-control, we are really showing how we have failed to magnify that pattern of wholeness which is ours to possess. Patience is love in action. Patience, with persistence, brings harmony, faith, hope, all spiritual virtues into our lives and into the lives of those we touch:

> . . . this *is* the day, the time, when all men must seek to be patient one with another, under all conditions and circumstances, that they may be one with Him who in patience endured all that we might have the access to the Father, through the patience, the love, the consciousness, shown in a material plane. Be faithful to that thou *knowest* to do . . . Let each live, then, as though they *expected* their concept of the Master Christ to *dine* with them today. What *would* ye have to offer as the fruits of thine own life, thine thoughts, thine acts, thine deeds? 262-25

Far from being a passive state of mind, true patience is a conscious activity that allows God's love, laws, and presence to come into our lives. When patience becomes our natural state of awareness (rather than simply what we should do) that consciousness becomes a portion of our being. With patience we can magnify God's virtues—our own pattern for wholeness—into our daily experiences. Each moment of our lives has the potential to move us closer toward who we really are in eternity. The readings would challenge us to be consistent. Be persistent. Be patient. In patience we come to an awareness of our soul.

THE OPEN DOOR

Behold, I stand at the door, and knock: if any man hear my voice, and open the door, I will come in to him, and will sup with him, and he with me. Revelation 3:20

MEDITATION AFFIRMATION

As the Father knoweth me, so may I know the Father, through the Christ Spirit, the door to the kingdom of the Father. Show Thou me the way. 262-27

THE OPEN DOOR

Introduction

Who, then, has learned to be truly cooperative one with another? Who has discerned self sufficient to know where self stands as in relationship with its fellow man? Who has set the ideal wholly in Him? Who magnifies the faith in the Father, in the Son, that it may be counted to them for righteousness? Who hath virtue and understanding, that they may magnify in their lives that fellowship which brings patience in the knowing of self to be growing in grace, in nurture and admonition of the Lord day by day? He, then, it is that opens the door that He may come in and sup with him! 262-28

Just as flowers make their surroundings more beautiful regardless of where they might find themselves, we too possess the ability, even the birthright, to brighten our own sphere of activity wherever we are. Each individual has the ability to make the world a better place, a more hopeful place in which others may live. It is not something out of reach, nor is it impossible even in the face of the world's turmoil, for God has prepared a way of meeting each of life's conditions:

> Consider the color, the beauty of the lily as it grows from its ugly muck, or the shrinking violet as it sends out its color, its odor to enrich even the very heart of God. Consider the rose as to how it unfolds with the color of the day, and with the opening itself to the sunshine, into the rain . . . Why won't people learn the lesson from them and grow in love and in beauty, in whatever may be their environ? Learn also from the flower that where thou art, ye,

too, may make that place more beautiful for your being there, whether it is in this or that or whatever place. 5122-1

Regardless of where we are in consciousness right now, a model of Wholeness, the pattern of the Christ Consciousness, stands ready to be manifested in our lives. It alone allows for the magnifying of soul activities in the earth as well as for the ultimate expression of our inner selves.

Essentially, the readings' lessons in personal spirituality were given as a means of awakening individuals to an awareness of this Christ Consciousness which longs to be expressed in the material world through each one of us. Our purpose, individually and collectively, is to be channels of God's activity in the earth. Although we may spend eons in pursuit only of material things, ultimately, we are to remember our heritage and our relationship with the Divine. This is the birthright of every soul. Regardless of where we may find ourselves right now, this manifestation of wholeness and this expression of *spirit in the earth* is our destiny.

Each one of us cannot help but feel an inner longing for something more. The readings suggest it is because the nature of humankind is that of seekers along the way. Though our confusion over what we are seeking may lead some to selfishness, constant struggles, or even to the feeling of being totally lost, it is God's will that we eventually succeed. We need only begin living the pattern of the Christ Consciousness, and turn to the Divine within:

Search then. For as He has given, "Seek and ye shall find; *knock* and it shall be opened unto you." *Who* will open? Where will it happen? *Within thine own conscience!* For *there* He has promised to meet thee! 1595-1

God's desire is that we might become selfless channels of His activity in the earth. This awareness of our
own potential for wholeness comes as a result of attunement to the Christ pattern. By attuning to His will and
then attempting to apply spiritual virtues in our daily
lives, soul forces are expressed in the physical world.
Even within the smallest acts of service we can begin to
see the glory of wholeness flowing forth from our lives.
Cayce suggests that the Divine stands ever-ready to
come into our lives; but ultimately, it is simply one's self
who must open the door to that awaiting consciousness:

> Do not, as was the admonition of old, say "Who
> will ascend into heaven that we may have a vision
> or a message, or who shall come from over the sea?"
> For, lo, it is in thine own heart, thine own con-
> science; and in the temple of thine own body has
> He promised to meet thee, and indeed will His
> Spirit bear witness with thy spirit. So he that looketh
> for a sign, or for a manifestation, other than that as
> may come in *His* way, seeketh in vain; for lo He
> standeth ever at the door of thine own heart. If ye
> will but open and let Him in, He will abide with
> thee, ever. 531-7

It is Christlike action, expressing the best we have to
offer within ourselves in our daily lives, which opens the
door to the activities of the Creator.

CULTIVATING A PERSONAL
RELATIONSHIP WITH GOD

Just as the Creator knows each one of us personally,
we too can come to know Him. This relationship is our
birthright, for we are His children. Since the dawn of
time, His desire has been that we each experience noth-

ing less than an ongoing awareness of His all-abiding presence. For that reason, we have been provided with a pattern of spirituality—one we can turn to in our every need, one which allows His love to flow through us into the lives of others:

> . . . "If ye will be my son, I will be thy God—If ye call, I will hear—Behold, I stand at the door and knock; I will enter, if ye ask." Then, these are not mere sayings! They are *facts*, truths, life itself! but the individual is not made aware of same through the material things nor material-mindedness; rather through spiritual-mindedness, as to purposes and activities of the soul in its lessons, its tenets that it has carried through its expressions in the earth. 1797-3

Spiritual-mindedness is living in attunement with our own pattern of wholeness. In fact, Cayce encouraged individuals to begin living so in accord with God's will that the "light of their lives" began to provide hope and encouragement to others. In order to cultivate this relationship with God, our challenge is to simply move our will in alignment with His. Essentially, the readings suggest three things which will help make this a practical experience in our everyday lives: prayer, meditation, and service.

Oftentimes, we might think of prayer as telling God what we need or want. However, Cayce believed that true prayer was not so much a petition for things as it was an expression of one's desire to gain an awareness of the Creator's will in our lives. In other words, prayer invites God to work through us. Meditation, on the other hand, is clearing aside all random thoughts so that we might become more attuned to some aspect of the Christ Consciousness within. It has also been called "attentive listening." In the language of the readings:

> For prayer is supplication for direction, for un-
> derstanding. Meditation is listening to the Divine
> within. 1861-19

> Then set definite periods for prayer; set definite
> periods for meditation. Know the difference be-
> tween each. Prayer, in short, is appealing to the Di-
> vine within self, the Divine from without self, and
> meditation is keeping still in body, in mind, in
> heart, listening, listening to the voice of thy Maker.
> 5368-1

From the readings perspective, we become a channel
of God's activity in the earth through spiritual attunement. That attunement leads, in turn, to service for others. By turning within, we gain an awareness of our
ultimate oneness with the Christ pattern, simply waiting to be awakened in our lives. That pattern is manifested as we assist anyone who comes our way to the best
of our abilities. As we do whatever we find to do in service, we are guided to the next step. We come to know
God by seeking to attune to His will for us in our interactions with others:

> Thus each entity, each individual, must realize
> this through the own attunement. Ye must *know* that
> He walks with thee. And, as has been indicated,
> there should come that experience of thy *hearing*
> His voice. When in attune ye will, ye do. For, as He
> has given, "I stand at the door and knock; if ye will
> open, I will enter." This is to be, this *is* then an indi-
> vidual experience—for each soul that seeks His
> presence. Think not that He has not heard, because
> it has not yet appeared so, or because thou hast not

yet heard Him save in the lives and the experiences of those thou hast helped. Seek not then thy way of manifestations, but more and more, "Here am I, Lord; use me, send me. Point the way that thou would have me go." This is a promise to thee, to each soul; yet each soul must of itself *find* the answer within self. For indeed the body is the temple of the living God. There He has promised to meet thee; there He does. And as thy body, thy mind, thy soul is attuned to that Divine as answers within, so may ye indeed be quickened to know His purpose; and ye may fill that purpose for which ye entered this experience . . . For, know—as He hath given— "Lo, I am with thee always, even unto the end." This is not a mere saying, but an awareness which one may find through that attuning through meditation, through prayer, through the opening of self for direction by Him. 69-4

Attuning to the Divine within enables individuals to become more aware of God's all-abiding presence.

Oftentimes, we have convinced ourselves that we are unworthy to know God, and have therefore neglected to seek Him. But we must realize that He has never condemned any of us, rather He has provided a means of coming to know ourselves and one another, a means that will help us to realize all we have ever desired is our relationship with Him. We come to manifest the Christ Consciousness, to live the Christ Spirit through prayer, meditation, and service. We come to know the Creator by attempting to manifest His attributes in the earth.

THE CHRIST CONSCIOUSNESS AS
THE DOOR TO GOD'S
ALL-ABIDING PRESENCE

God desires that we seek His presence, becoming a channel of His love unto others. He continually seeks to be in communion with us, although we may often have a hard time listening. The first study group was told that as they manifested the Christ Consciousness in their daily experiences, they opened the door to His presence (262-121). As this consciousness (*the awareness of our Oneness with God*) is expressed in our thoughts and our deeds, we become a channel of God's blessings to others. Cayce's admonition was that we become light-bearers to those who are in darkness.

Unfortunately, human nature is such that we might easily find ourselves preaching to others what we think we have come to know, rather than attempting to simply *live* that awareness of our spiritual nature in the earth. With right-thought and right-action, we can bring the awareness of God's presence into every one of our activities:

Then may ye as seekers of the way, may ye that have come seeking to know, to experience, to *feel* that presence of the Christ Consciousness within thine own breast, within thine own experience, *open* the door of thy heart! For He stands ready to enter, to those who will bid Him enter. He comes not unbidden, but as ye seek ye find; as ye knock it is opened. As ye live the life is the awareness of His closeness, of His presence, thine. Then, again as He gave, "Love ye one another," thus fulfilling *all* that is in the purpose of His entrance into materiality; to replace hate and jealousy and those things that make one afraid, with love and hope and joy. So be ye then as His children . . . 5749-10

Each of us must turn within so that the pattern of spirit may enter into our lives. God-mindedness is achieved not by force nor by persuading others to see things the way we do, rather it comes as we make our wills subservient to God's will for us. All thoughts of self-ishness must be replaced with the desire to be used as a channel of blessings to others. Whenever we find our-selves in a self-centered frame of mind we cannot help but experience lack or even feel cheated in life. However, when we place another's well-being before our own, we become more receptive to the good that is trying to find its way through us:

> In giving that as may be helpful to each in gain-ing an inspiration—this, to be sure, must come from within, and each may only be directed as to a way or means in which each may give. Then as ye give ye may receive that inspiration, that blessing. This ye have realized in thy efforts and in thy pur-poses; though the desire has been at times to gain knowledge. This is not amiss, *if* the knowledge is ap-plied in such a way as to become beneficial, or a helpful influence in the lives of others; bringing them, through thine own principle, thine own pur-poses, thine own desire, to an awakening to those abilities which lie within—where each may attune self to the consciousness of the Christ within . . . All are children of that Creative Force, God. All are brethren, then, with thy Lord; who has promised, "Lo, I stand at the door and knock. If ye open, I will come in and sup with thee." Give thanks for that thou hast—the opportunity, the day, the period in the experience of the earth, when ye may raise thy voice in praise to Him. 281-56

As we become more aware of our inner spiritual pat-

tern, we gain deeper insights into how we might express
it in the world. Only by applying what little we may know
day by day is the spirit quickened, enabling us to experience attunement and at-onement with Him. And in the
process of discovering our own spiritual nature, we begin to recognize each individual as a fellow seeker along
the way.

JESUS AS ELDER BROTHER

As mentioned previously, the Edgar Cayce material
presents the life of Jesus as an example for every soul in
the earth. The knowledge of His own spiritual nature and
the manifestation of the Christ Consciousness led to the
awareness that "I and my Father are one." (John 10:30)
But more than just an awareness of His relationship to
the Divine, the readings suggest that Jesus lived in a
manner where He placed others' needs before His own
and chose instead to be of service to all. By so doing, He
became the "Good Shepherd" of all God's children, taking upon Himself the mission of assisting each one of us
in finding our way back to the Creator—regardless of our
religious background. Jesus understood that His own life
was to be a channel of God's activity unto others. Therefore, whenever we feel confused as to our own direction,
oftentimes the answer can be found by assisting another
in finding their own way.

Cayce advised everyone that during moments of confusion, doubt, or problems which seemed insurmountable, Jesus, as Elder Brother, stood ready to assist them:

As to how to meet each problem: Take it to Jesus!
He *is* thy answer. He is Life, Light and Immortality.
He is Truth, and is thy Elder Brother. Not as to who
will ascend into heaven to bring thee a message, or
who would go over the sea that ye might know of

Him, but He is in thine own heart; for He hath given, "Behold I stand at the door and knock." Will ye open and let Him in? For in *Him* is strength, not in the law, not in the man, not in the multitudes of men, nor of conditions or circumstance. For He ruleth, He maketh them—every one. For hath it not been given or told thee, hath it not been known in thine experience that "He is the Word, He maketh all that was made, and without Him there was nothing made that was made"? And He *liveth* in the hearts and the souls of those who seek to do His biddings. This, then, is not idealistic—but an *ideal!* "What would Jesus have me do" regarding every question in thy relationships with thy fellow man, in thy home, in thy problems day by day. This rather should be the question, rather than "What shall I do?" 1326-1

When Jesus stated, "I am the way, the truth, and the life: no man cometh unto the Father, but by me"(John 14:6), he was stating that His own life was an example for each one of us, and only by living in accord with that pattern—the outward manifestation of the Christ Consciousness within—could we come into a full awareness of our true relationship with the Divine. Essentially, that pattern calls for an attitude of selfless service, becoming a channel of blessings unto others.

SELFLESSNESS AS AN ATTITUDE

According to the readings, depending upon our choices and activities, we either become servants to our own desires or servants to the need of others. For most of us, however, the greatest fault we face is that of selfishness. For that reason, we must constantly strive to become aware of our purpose for being in the earth.

Cayce frequently advised individuals, "Do not become weary in well-doing":

> Then, today, we are to answer within our individual consciousness, "Am I my brother's keeper?" Not "What does the world owe me?" but "What contribution can I, as an individual soul seeking God, seeking to know His face, make that may hasten the day of the Lord?" For we as individuals, as we look about us, realize more and more that indeed we live and move and have our being in Him—and we are becoming mindful also *of* "from whence we came." And we realize that as He has given, "If ye will be my people, I will be thy God" applies to me, to you, to each soul that has been blessed with the consciousness, the awareness of life. For life itself in all its forms and phases is indeed a manifestation of that we worship as God. 3976-22

It is important to remember that "selflessness" does not mean disregarding self or thinking of one's self as being worthless. It is not becoming a doormat. True selflessness allows the individuality of one's soul to become a channel for the activities of the Christ. Everyone has the capacity to be used in this manner if they would but recognize their opportunities, day by day, in their interactions with others:

> Know it is in the little things, not by thunderous applause, not by the ringing of bells, nor the blowing of whistles, that the Son of Man comes— humble, gently, kind, meek, lowly—for "He that is the greatest among you serveth all." This is the attitude. Yes, it is well that others in the home, others of the connections and associations, have their share also. Ask them, that they assist in the problems,

even as He asks that you open the door of your heart, that He may enter, to give them the opportunity also for a part of the service. These are the manners, the ways. For as He has given, "In my Father's house are many mansions." In the problems with the daily tasks, the daily obligations, there are many opportunities—and thus in His house. For thy body is indeed the temple of the living God, and there He has promised to meet thee. He has said, "If ye call, I will hear—and will answer speedily." Let thine own conscience then bear witness with those activities of the day, that ye do walk and talk oft in prayer to thy Lord and Master, thy Brother, who has given thee a share in the glory of the Kingdom of God, by thy merely being patient and kind to others who are hard to deal with at times. But in prayer, in hope, in desire, you may find in Him the help needed. 3161-1

Service to others is the greatest service to God. Whenever self is put aside, the spirit is allowed to shine through us. We demonstrate the presence of God in our lives and express our inner pattern of wholeness whenever we reach out to another. As the readings suggest, the greatest act of service is not necessarily anything more than just being kind, just being loving, just renewing hope in the life of one who may have given up. In this manner, we share with others that same joy, peace, and happiness that He would share with us.

CONCLUSION

Regardless of who we are, or where we find ourselves, we have a connection to one another. We are all children of the same God. Deep within us we possess a consciousness of His force, power, love, and presence. That presence is manifested in the world around us by doing the very best that we know to do. By becoming channels of His love and by being of service to those we contact, the world becomes a better place for our being a part of it. Meditation, prayer, and service move us beyond the confusion of our own problems and difficulties and enable us to open the door to His all-abiding presence.

If we would be His people, He will be our God. The relationship we possess with the Creator has been our birthright from the foundation of the world. The awareness of our oneness with Him will come as we manifest the Christ Consciousness in our daily lives. He stands at the door and knocks, for we have been called for a service. The Edgar Cayce readings implore us to allow His presence into our lives. From this day forth, let us seek to manifest the activity of the Creator in the earth:

. . . the door is through the life, the spirit of the life—not the man, but the spirit as manifest in the Christ Consciousness in the material world. So, as each do manifest in their daily walks in and before men with that consciousness as the standard, so may the door be opened for that entity, that soul, to so grow and magnify that spirit to the glorifying of the Father, losing self in the service to others, that in the earth His name may be established forever. 262-27

LESSON NINE

IN HIS PRESENCE

And I will walk among you, and will be your God, and ye shall be my people. Leviticus 26:12

MEDITATION AFFIRMATION

Our Father, who art in heaven, may Thy kingdom come in earth through Thy presence in me, that the light of Thy word may shine unto those that I meet day by day. May Thy presence in my brother be such that I may glorify Thee. May I so conduct my own life that others may know Thy presence abides with me, and thus glorify Thee.

262-30

In His Presence

Introduction

Let not the cares of the world disturb thee, for those things that are of the earth-earthy pass away—even as the mist before the noonday sun. He that hath found the Lord and taken Him *as his companion shall melt away the cares even as the sun. Keep in the way that thou knowest to go, for it is right in the eyes of the Lord. Comfort the weak; cherish the downtrodden; give praise for thy strength in the Lord. Through thee much good may come to many . . . in the kind word here, a word fitly spoken there. For here a little, there a little and the growth is from within; and will shine out to those—if ye do take Him as thy companion.* 473-2

With the living *of that given all will come to the knowledge, to the understanding of, we are all* in *His presence whether we acknowledge it in the present or not; for, as has been given, it is in Him we live and move and have our being . . .* 262-32

In the same manner that a loving parent shows no favoritism to one child over another, God loves each of us equally. He does not take sides in religious differences, or political battles, or discussions of dogma. His desire is simply for each of us to express the full awareness of the *living spirit* in the earth. Though we may be separated by vast distances, by creeds, by race, or even by ignorance, we are all part of the same Whole. Each of us is "a corpuscle in the body of God; thus a co-creator with Him." (2794-3)

We have often imagined God as being "up there" or "out there" or only in a particular place of worship.

Sometimes, we give thought to the existence of Him only because it happens to be our day of worship, or perhaps because we have a particular need. Even though we are always in His presence, we forget to open ourselves to the awareness that He is always in ours:

For man remains in the presence of same, ever; for His presence abideth. He is nearer than thy hand, than thy mind, if ye will but take hold upon Him. 1257-1

The truth of the matter is that the Creator cannot be separated from His creation, even though much of humankind has been unable to fully understand this fact due to our own lack of awareness. Each manifestation of Creation is part of the Whole. God is the Creative Force underlying everything. He is at the foundation of all that exists.

One of the promises in the Cayce readings states that because of our heritage and our true relationship with the Divine, there will come a time in our development when our awareness of Him is never apart from who we think we are. In fact, an undergirding principle within the entire body of the Edgar Cayce information deals with the imminence of God: *the Creator is everywhere at all times and in all places!* As long as we believe He is apart from us, we are forgetting our birthright. We must remember that we are Children of God, spiritual beings who would seek to manifest our Creator's attributes in the earth. His presence is everlasting—the awareness of that presence grows as we seek to cultivate a relationship with Him, attempting to serve as a channel of His blessings:

Seek not then thy way of manifestations, but more and more, "Here am I, Lord; use me, send me.

Point the way that thou would have me go." This is a promise to thee, to each soul; yet each soul must of itself *find* the answer within self. For indeed the body is the temple of the living God. There He has promised to meet thee; there He does. And as thy body, thy mind, thy soul is attuned to that Divine as answers within, so may ye indeed be quickened to know His purpose; and ye may fill that purpose for which ye entered this experience. 69-4

Our destiny is to come to an awareness of our true relationship with God. Just what are we doing in order to move our consciousness in that direction?

CULTIVATING THE AWARENESS OF HIS PRESENCE

The Cayce information suggests that whenever we feel disconnected from God, we need to make no mistake about who moved. It is not that His presence is missing, rather we lack an awareness of that Presence. As spiritual beings in the earth, our challenge seems to be one in which we need do those things that can facilitate our being continually reawakened to the presence of the Divine within.

Sometimes we mistakenly believe that the only way we can become spiritual is to "get away from it all." But it is not in withdrawing from the world that we fulfill our destiny, rather it is in striving for balance:

Take time to be holy, but take time to play also. Take time to rest, time to recuperate; for thy Master, even in the pattern in the earth, took time to rest, took time to be apart from others, took time to meditate and pray, took time to attend a wedding, to give time to attend a funeral; took time to attend those awakenings from death and took time to minister to all. 5246-1

In an effort to explain how an individual could come into a living awareness of the Christ Consciousness, one person was given this analogy:

> . . . how, when and in what way does an individual become aware of the laws pertaining to the construction of a sentence in English? How, where, when, in what manner does an individual learn the rule of spelling a word? By the meditating upon same, by seeing, visualizing, acting. And then the *awareness* of same is manifested by the manner in which the individual puts same into practice in conjunction or association with its fellow man. The knowledge may be existent, the awareness in self may be present; but if the individual does not apply same in its associations . . . it becomes of none effect. 272-9

In other words, we cannot expect to *feel* the ongoing presence of God's love until we have attempted to work on our own attunement and then apply what we have learned. In fact, attunement and application are at the heart of the Cayce information on spiritual transformation.

Repeatedly, the readings advised individuals to work with prayer and meditation consistently and persistently—in other words, *every day!* In addition to facilitating personal attunement, in part the reason is because there is a difference between believing in God and having a continuous awareness of Him. Meditation and prayer help to build that consciousness of His all-abiding presence. In the language of the readings:

Then, in making practical or concrete activity of the entity in its experience, first enter in as through the meditative forces within self; through the purifying of the body, of the mind, that it may be one and in accord, in attune with the Creative Forces from within; setting the ideal in Him who has promised to meet thee in the holy of holies, in the temple of thy soul, in thy own body-consciousness. Thus does the self, the *I am* become aware of that presence. 261-15

Next to attunement, the most important thing we can do to help facilitate personal transformation is application—just doing what one knows to do day by day. Although we may sometimes feel as though we don't know "what to do," one suggestion is to attempt to carry out all of our day's events as though our Creator was present. The irony is that of course He *is* with us, but the activity helps to remind ourselves of that all-abiding Presence. Essentially, the readings advised individuals who wanted to become more spiritual to begin acting more in accord with the things of the spirit. Whatever we consistently apply in our lives grows to be a part of our consciousness to such an extent that it becomes our automatic and natural response. It is simply line upon line, precept upon precept, step by step, that we cultivate the awareness of His presence:

To be sure it will require time, patience, persistence and consistency. It will also be necessary for the mental and spiritual attitudes to be in that way of never condemning self or others, but rather looking to that power which lies within to have every atom of the body and mind attuned to creative energies as in the Christ Consciousness, of His abiding presence with thee. 3694-1

As has been given, "Do that thou *knowest* to *do
today,* and *then* the next step may be given thee" . . .
ye come more and more, by such living, to the
awareness of His presence abiding with thee! Not
unto vainglorying, not unto self-consciousness; but
rather that "Here am I, Lord, use me. Let *me* be that
channel of blessing to *someone today;* that *Thy* love,
Thy glory, Thy oneness, may be the greater manifested in not only my experience but those that I
contact day by day." 601-11

From Cayce's perspective, we do not "go" to heaven
instead we "grow" in consciousness until our activities
and our thoughts reflect our heritage as Children of God.
In one respect, our purpose in life is to simply become
so attuned to spirit and to the consciousness of His presence that we bring Heaven into the earth.

BEING A CHANNEL OF HIS PRESENCE

The Cayce readings suggest that our daily prayer
should be "Let *me* be that channel of blessing to *someone today.*" (601-11) One woman was told (3003) to begin each day by praying three times for God's direction
and guidance, and then to listen and attune to His
answer. If we allow ourselves to be open to the possibility, God will use us however He thinks best. From this
perspective, the purpose of each day is to become a better channel of His love to whomever we contact. Ultimately, through attunement, application, and free will,
we manifest the awareness of the Christ Consciousness
from within until we become a channel of loving service:

For know, there is that awareness that should be
in self, that the very fact ye are conscious of thy ac-

tivity in the material plane should be evidence that
thy Father-God hath need of thy service in the
earth, and that through the present activity ye are
given the opportunity to be a channel of blessing to
someone. For, to obtain the consciousness and
awareness of coming into His presence, or as one
would call to heaven, it will be as if it were leaning
on the arm of someone ye have tried to help. For as
ye do it unto thy brother, ye do it unto thy Maker.
Know they are immutable laws. God is, and ye as a
daughter, as a servant of the most high God are His
handmaid. Then act like it! 5177-1

We must continually prepare ourselves to be aware of
His presence, and to give the knowledge of that presence
to others in our daily lives. In other words, Cayce would
ask, "How many people have you lifted in consciousness
today?" How many individuals have we made to feel better because of our presence? When our thoughts and our
actions are in accord with the inner pattern of wholeness, we allow His attributes to manifest through us—
positively affecting even those around us.

In a very beautiful passage from one reading, Cayce's
biographer, Thomas Sugrue, author of *There Is a River*,
was told that the destiny of every soul had been beautifully demonstrated by Jesus, the ultimate example of
love and service to others. Our Elder Brother gave us an
example of how we might best manifest the ongoing
awareness of God's presence. Sugrue was told that this
Christ Consciousness could be (and would be) manifested in each of our own lives, as follows:

Not in mighty deeds of valor, not in the exalta-
tion of thy knowledge or thy power; but in the
gentleness of the things of the spirit: love, kindness,
long-suffering, patience; these thy brother hath

shown thee that thou, applying them in thy asso-
ciations with thy fellow man day by day, here a little,
there a little, may become one with Him as He has
destined that thou shouldst be! Wilt thou separate
thyself? For there be nothing in heaven, in earth, in
hell, that may separate thee from the love of thy
God, of thy brother, save thine own self! Then, be
up and doing . . . 849-11

Each of us must "be up and doing," becoming living
examples of what we profess to believe. Those individuals who best serve as channels of His presence are simply those who have opened their hearts to let Him in,
for regardless of where we find ourselves, He is always
near.

OUR WALK WITH GOD

Sometimes this principle that God is everywhere can
be challenging. We may not feel worthy to recognize the
awareness of His presence within us and around us, or
we might find it difficult to acknowledge His presence
within individuals with whom we have been having difficulty. However, the readings offer the startling statement that "ye have not begun to think straight until ye
are able to see in the life of those whom ye utterly dis-
like, something ye would worship in thy Maker." (3575-
2) This suggests that there is good, even *godliness* within
every individual, even though there may be times when
we find it extremely challenging to recognize it. And yet,
our search for God requires that we attempt to become
aware of His presence at all times and in every circumstance.

Each of us is made in the image of our Creator. However, that image is one of spirit, not physicality. Too often we allow ourselves to associate entirely with the

things of the material world. By so doing, we can easily forget that the physical body is simply the vehicle through which we can manifest His presence in the earth. The frequently quoted *"Spirit is the life, mind is the builder, and the physical is the result"* should remind us that all things originate at the level of spirit. It is at this level that we need to direct our focus and attunement. Regardless of where we find ourselves in consciousness right now, ultimately the truth of our relationship with the Divine (and His all-abiding presence) will become the focal point of our awareness:

> The soul, then, must return—*will* return—to its Maker. It is a portion of the Creative Force, which is energized into activity even in materiality, in the flesh. Yet it may, with thine own understanding and thine own manifestations, come to be as a portion of that thou bringest in thy love into thy fellow man, for thy Father-God, for thy activity to be *one* with Him in those realms of activity and experience that ye *are* aware of His presence, of His abiding love, of His abiding faith *in* thee motivating thee in thy activities in every direction. Then, just being kind, just being patient, just showing love for thy fellow man; *that* is the manner in which an individual works *at* becoming aware of the consciousness of the Christ Spirit. 272-9

Sometimes we may feel that possessing an ongoing awareness of God is not even possible, but Cayce reminded a group of his supporters that His presence was close at hand. In fact, He longs to be in our presence:

> How beautiful the face, how lovely the clouds! In His presence abide; ye *every one* of you who are before Him just now. His face is turned toward thee,

His heart and hand is offered you. Will ye not accept Him just now? How glorious the knowledge
of His presence should awaken in the hearts of
you, for He is *lonely* without thee; for He has
called each of you by name. Will ye fail Him now?
254-76

Each day we have another opportunity to manifest an
attribute of the Creator in the earth. Although we may
not feel worthy, we must remember that the Divine is not
separate from us—it is a portion of us all. Each individual
possesses a kinship with God. It is not that God has forgotten to abide with any of us, rather it is that we have
overlooked the truth of His presence. As we press on-
ward, doing what we know to do through attunement
and service, we gain an understanding that we can become an integral portion of His activity in the earth. As
we live in the knowledge of His presence, His light can
shine forth in our words, in our thoughts, and in our
deeds—throughout the very fiber of our being. All that is
required of us is the "try." God will provide the increase,
as well as the next step in our direction.

CONCLUSION

The Christ pattern, our own model for wholeness,
stands ready to manifest in our lives. There is nothing in
all the universe that may separate us from an awareness
of this Presence except for ourselves. For He is the same
yesterday, today, and forever, and will be our God if we
will be His people. As His spiritual children, we are His
Companions and Co-Creators. We become more and
more aware of this all-abiding Presence as self is set
aside. As we turn within, we discover the awareness of
His presence and the realization of our ultimate oneness
with Him. As we seek Him and His will, our faith is

strengthened, our hope renewed, and our path made clear. The Creator is God of each of us. The knowledge of His presence is within our grasp, for it is within our very selves. *God is everywhere!* The search for God leads to this one simple fact: *there is not a part of God's Creation that exists without His full presence.* We are His spiritual Children and He has need of us:

> "Thou shalt love the Lord thy God with all thy heart, thy mind, thy body; thy neighbor as thyself." This as He gave is the whole law. There is none above that. And ye may, as He has promised, become aware in thy own consciousness of His abiding presence, by the awarenesses that may come to thee as ye meditate, as ye pray from day to day. Ask and He will give. For as ye walk, as ye talk with Him, ye become aware of His presence abiding with thee. For this purpose ye came into this experience; that ye might *glorify* that consciousness, that awareness of His presence, of His Spirit abiding with thee. 1348-1

Our bodies and our lives were fashioned to be a dwelling place for His spirit. Day by day we are given the opportunity to become aware of God's presence and to share that presence with one another. We have the opportunity to magnify His attributes in the earth. It is our responsibility as well as our birthright. What could be more beautiful than the promise of His presence abiding with us just now?

> Love His ways. Keep in His ways. This alone may bring to thine mind, thine soul, thine body, that which will make for soul awareness of His presence abiding with thee. Let the light, even the light of Him, open thine heart, open thine mind, that He

may come in. For, He standeth near. He will direct, He will bring cheer to thee . . . Make thy will His will. Let His will be thy will—now. 378-46

God would walk in the earth among His children through us.

LESSON TEN

THE CROSS AND THE CROWN

But love ye your enemies, and do good, and lend, hoping for nothing again; and your reward shall be great, and ye shall be the children of the Highest ... Be ye therefore merciful, as your Father also is merciful. Judge not, and ye shall not be judged: condemn not, and ye shall not be condemned: forgive, and ye shall be forgiven: Give, and it shall be given unto you ... For with the same measure that ye mete withal it shall be measured to you again.

Luke 6:35-38

MEDITATION AFFIRMATION

Our Father, our God, as we approach that that may give us a better insight of what He bore in the cross, what His glory may be in the crown, may Thy blessings—as promised through Him—be with us as we study together in His name. 262-34

THE CROSS AND THE CROWN

Introduction

...in the lesson The Cross, The Crown, *there is made the definite stand of the activities of an entity, that must come to stand as that which is first and foremost in the minds mentally, the minds spiritually, of each entity. As given, "I am determined to know nothing among men save Jesus, the Christ, and him crucified." So, He, with the cross, represents something in the experience of every entity in their activities through the earth, and has led in all of the experiences of thought in* any *of the presented forms of truth in the earth, and comes at last to the cross ... so must the central theme, the basis of each individual's approach be: Not "What is my cross?" which is the usual first question in every* material *mind, but rather "How may I with His aid best* meet *my cross, in my approach to the crown of righteousness?"...* 262-34

For, know that each soul is a free-willed individual, and chooses the way and the application. For it is either the co-worker with God in creation—and creative then in its attitude, in its thought, in its application of tenets and truths day by day; or in attune with that which is at variance, and thus besetting or putting stumbling blocks in the way of others along the way. 2549-1

The Creator intended man to be a companion with Him. Whether in heaven or in the earth or in whatever consciousness, a companion with the Creator. How many [lifetimes/ experiences] will it require for thee to be able to be a companion with Creative Forces wherever you are? 416-18

Throughout all of the Cayce material on spirituality, the lesson on the Cross and the Crown is one of the most promising and challenging. It is promising because of the information it presents on the destiny of the soul. It can also appear to be provocative, and may be one of the most emotionally charged sets of materials—one with which there can be a great degree of misunderstanding. In fact, two members of the original study group withdrew from the group because of the information contained within this very lesson. What is most challenging to our understanding, perhaps, is the material which discusses the dynamics of reincarnation.

In spite of the confusion that can be associated with the concept, reincarnation is not destiny. It does not eliminate the God-given power of free will. It does not undermine the mission of Jesus, nor does it overlook the power of grace. From Cayce's perspective, the process of reincarnation is simply the manner in which each of us goes through a series of lifetimes enabling us to meet the consequences of our previous choices. Ultimately we will learn that only those choices which are in keeping with the things of the spirit, or the pattern of the Christ Consciousness, are what we truly desire at the soul level. Although this entire concept may be the most challenging to deal with, it is not even the core assumption contained within the Cross and the Crown. The heart of the lesson is simply as follows:

Each of us have "crosses" (or habit patterns or desires) that stand between us and a full awareness of our relationship with the Divine. Whether from the present or from the past, these crosses are of our own making and must be overcome before we can reach the full manifestation of the Christ Consciousness in the earth. The only way we can manifest the Christ Consciousness is through complete and willing selflessness—allowing self to be used as a channel of God's love. The first individual to demonstrate complete selflessness and manifestation of this Divine Consciousness was Jesus, our Elder Brother. In other words, Jesus overcame the world by allowing the presence of God to flow so completely through Him, that He became at-one with God. This at-onement is the destiny for every single soul:

> As has been given, man was made a little lower than the angels, yet with that power to become one with God, while the angel remains the angel. In the life, then, of Jesus we find the oneness made manifest through the ability to overcome all of the temptations of the flesh, and the desires of same, through making the *will one with the Father.* For as we find, oft did He give to those about Him those injunctions, "Those who have seen me have seen the Father," and in man, He, the Son of Man, became one with the Father. Man, through the same channel, may reach that perfection . . . 900-16

The process whereby we move toward at-onement and wholeness is not only grounded in attunement and application and strengthened by our spiritual motivation (or ideal), but it also through the interconnected dynamics of free will, karma, and grace. Only by attempting to understand the activities of each, while learning—at the same time—to set all selfishness aside, can we even hope to achieve our goal of becoming a perfect channel of His love:

> Be patient, be kind. Be gentle in thy ministerings day by day; for though there may come those periods when the burden seems heavy, and the light fades in the life, yet he that is faithful unto the end shall wear the crown. Keep the fires of love burning in thy hearts day by day, for the love of God is manifested in the earth through those that are just kind one to another. 281-17

AN OVERVIEW OF CAYCE'S
APPROACH TO REINCARNATION

Just what is reincarnation? It is the process whereby each of us goes through a series of lifetimes for the purpose of spiritual growth and soul development. Cayce's viewpoint *does not* include the concept of transmigration, which states that it is possible for human beings to be born again as animals. From the standpoint of the Edgar Cayce material, souls incarnate only in human bodies.

Cayce's approach to reincarnation provides a practical framework that enables individuals to see how their choices, thoughts, and actions have created the substance of their lives. Simply stated, we draw to us exactly what we need to experience in order to meet the consequences of our previous choices. We learn both from our "mistakes" as well as from our "successes." Rather than being predestined or fatalistic in nature, this activity provides for the fairness of the Creator which does not exist without the reincarnation concept.

> *Q. If a soul fails to improve itself, what becomes of it?*
>
> A. That's why the reincarnation, why it reincarnates; that it *may* have the opportunity. Can the will of man continue to defy its Maker? 826-8

Cayce was familiar with some of the misunderstandings regarding the dynamics of reincarnation. From his perspective, any approach that did not take into account the dynamics of grace, free will, and karma was shortsighted. Even to this day, many individuals misinterpret reincarnation as a fatalistic journey through life because of "karma." This is definitely not Cayce's approach. From the standpoint of the readings, *karma is only memory,* it

is not destiny. These memories are generally unconscious and influence our abilities, our faults, even our
relationships with others. For example, an immediate
affinity toward an individual is as likely to be "karmic" as
an immediate animosity toward someone might be. But
even in the midst of this unconscious memory, an
individual's free will determines how he or she chooses
to respond to that information. The choices we make
determine the next set of potential experiences we encounter.

If there is only one life to live, why is it that so many
appear to have been given every advantage while others
seem to have been treated unfairly? Surely, an all-loving
God could not be responsible for such disharmony.
Therefore, if we do have free will, and if God does not
randomly choose to give some of His children advan-
tages over others, then *ultimately* our previous choices
must somehow be responsible for where we find ourselves right now:

> As an individual in any experience, in any period,
> uses that of which it (the soul or entity) is conscious
> in relation to the laws of the Creative Forces, so does
> that soul, that entity, develop towards—what? A
> companionship with the Creative influence! 5753-1

> For each soul, each entity, *constantly* meets self.
> And if each soul would but understand, those hard-
> ships which are accredited much to others are
> caused most by self. *Know* that in those you are
> meeting *thyself!* 845-4

The ways in which we decide to "meet self"—one experience and one choice at a time—will determine the
life we lead. Therefore, our free will relates to the activity
of *choice*. With our free will we can turn the challenges

that life presents us into opportunities for growth *or* we can see them as obstacles and unfair trials. Grace is the activity of the Creator which occurs whenever we choose to allow God to manifest His presence in our lives. For this reason, the influence of grace somehow supersedes the activities of both karma and free will.

The goal of gaining an understanding of reincarnation is not to discover who we were in the past, for it is not what we once did that counts; rather, it is *what we will do about what we know to do today.* Ultimately, all experiences will be for our own good and for our own growth, and everything we have drawn to us is of our own creation. It does not come as a self-imposed punishment, rather as a tool for coming to know our true selves and our ultimate relationship with the Creator. The earth is our classroom:

In the studies, then, know *where* ye are going . . . to find that ye only lived, died and were buried under the cherry tree in Grandmother's garden does not make thee one whit [a] better neighbor, citizen, mother or father! But to know that ye spoke unkindly and suffered for it, and in the present may correct it by being righteous—*that* is worthwhile! 5753-2

From Cayce's perspective, each of us has lessons in soul growth that need to be learned. We can utilize our free will to allow grace into our lives so that those lessons can be met in accordance with His will, or we can simply let karma bring those same lessons into our experience in ways which will be more difficult and challenging.

JESUS AS PATTERN AND
ELDER BROTHER

As God's children we are all peers; one child is not greater or more special somehow than another. And yet, we do have an example of our own inner pattern of Wholeness—the Christ Consciousness come to full manifestation. As such, our Elder Brother became this pattern, one who is willing to assist us on our own path back to the Creator. By choosing to live a life in attunement with this pattern, we will no longer be totally subject to our own karmic memory and can instead become more readily open to the activities of grace operating in our life. After all, we are joint heirs with Jesus:

There has also come a teacher who was bold enough to declare himself as the son of the living God. He set no rules of appetite. He set no rules of ethics, other than "As ye would that men should do to you, do ye even so to them," and to know "Inasmuch as ye do it unto the least of these, thy brethren, ye do it unto thy Maker." He declared that the kingdom of heaven is within each individual entity's consciousness, to be attained, to be aware of— through meditating upon the fact that God is the Father of every soul. Jesus, the Christ, is the mediator. And in Him, and in the study of His examples in the earth, is *life*—and that ye may have it more abundantly. He came to demonstrate, to manifest, to give life and light to all. Here, then, ye find a friend, a brother, a companion. As He gave, "I call ye not servants, but brethren." For, as many as believe, to them He gives power to become the children of God, the Father; joint heirs with this Jesus, the Christ, in the knowledge and in the awareness of this presence abiding ever with those who set this ideal before them. What, then, is this as an ideal? As concerning thy fellow man, He gave, "As ye would that others do to you, do ye even so to them," take no thought, worry not, be not overanxious about the body. For He knoweth what ye have need of. In the place thou art, in the consciousness in which ye find yourself, is that which is *today, now,* needed for thy greater, thy better, thy more wonderful unfoldment. 357-13

When Jesus said, "I am the way, the truth, and the life," (John 14:6) it was not a call to recognize him as a god; but rather an opportunity for us to realize that His life could serve as an example for each of us. Regardless of our religious background, in Jesus's life the way of service is made clear. By following His example we need not stumble. He showed the way back to the Creator and Wholeness, so that it would be easier for us to follow. In His life can be found the embodiment of truth throughout the ages. The new commandment that he demonstrated was that we love one another.

In Scripture we read, "For I determined not to know any thing among you, save Jesus Christ, and him crucified." (I Corinthians 2:2) This was not written from a perspective of religious conversion, but rather with the understanding of how Jesus' life of service embodies the lifestyle through which each of us can find the way back to our relationship with God. Ultimately, it is only by the giving of ourselves through the pattern of service that we will attain our ultimate goal:

Keep the self in such a manner as to be circumspect in thine own consciousness. Be true to self, making for those activities that bear the fruits of the spirit; just being kind, just being gentle, just being patient, just showing fellowship, just showing brotherly love; just bearing witness in thy walks, thy acts, thy understandings unto thy fellow man. And ye shall know Him face to face. For He hath promised to being to such the *remembrances* from the foundations of the earth, of the world, of the universe. For thou wert in the beginning, even as He. 261-15

Jesus became at-one with the Father, hence able to point the way back to the Creator, the Source from whence we all came. For that reason, He was given power over all the earth. In bearing the cross, he said, "It is finished" (John 19:30)—at long last the spirit of God had been manifested in the earth. He showed the way to live a perfect life in spite of the trials and conditions that may surround us day by day. Through Jesus we are shown what divine love can do when it is allowed to work through us.

WHY IS IT NECESSARY THAT HUMAN BEINGS SUFFER?

Since the dawn of Creation, much of the world has been lost in the misconception that happiness and fulfillment could be found in pursuit of things which were out of harmony with God's laws. We are confronted daily by crosses arising from our own participation in this misperception. We continue to bear these challenges because we have not yet learned to give complete expression to our soul faculties. Even though our ultimate state is divine, we continually find ourselves subject to the material laws which we have drawn to us:

So may ye, in thy dealings with the problems that arise in thy daily life; and as ye analyze from that as may be visioned or meditated upon, from activities in the varied earthly experiences. For, ye realize that ye *are* meeting thine old self—yea, thy old friends, thy old enemies. 2174-2

Just as our Elder Brother, we are all on our way back to at-onement with the Creator. From the readings' perspective, those things which prevent us from becoming channels of His love must be dealt with. In our own lives, the crosses we bear include our trials, our suffering, even our challenges. Eventually, we will discover that we must meet every consequence of our thoughts, words, and deeds through karma—drawing to us experiences that, when met, will leave us with the necessary awareness— *or* through grace—calling upon the promises of our Elder Brother and receiving that awareness without always having to stumble through each of life's problems. Rather than seeing our challenges as suffering, we have the opportunity to see each lesson as an opportunity for soul growth, moving us ever closer to Him:

Know this, learn this well: God is mindful of thee and will not allow thee to suffer beyond that ye are able to bear in thy body-mind, that ye may prepare the soul for the closer walk with Him. Remember this also, that though He were the Son, yet learned He obedience through the things which He suffered. Thou art not greater; thou art not better than He. 5348-1

OUR OWN PATH
TOWARD WHOLENESS

Edgar Cayce believed that the cross was also symbolic of that which had to be dealt with and overcome in every individual's life. Our crosses are only misunderstandings and misapplications of God's laws and can be overcome

through service, humility, patience, forgiveness, determination, and love. Regardless of what personal challenges we might face—regardless of the personal crosses
we may bear—our Elder Brother left us with words of
encouragement: "In the world ye shall have tribulation:
but be of good cheer; I have overcome the world." (John
16:33) Jesus overcame the world through each of His own
experiences. In simplest terms, He overcame the necessity for individuals to be subject only to karma. Instead,
He made the path of grace more easily accessible to each
of us and our own relationship with God more clearly
defined:

> Then, as one holds that consciousness, as one
> sets self to become one with that understanding
> necessary for the awakening of all forces and
> sources of activity within the physical conscious-
> ness as related both to the mental and material
> conditions in the life, so does there come within
> self that awareness *of* that position held, that posi-
> tion one finds self within, and so is there given—
> through those promises that are in Him, by Him
> and *through* Him—that necessary for one to meet
> those things in their daily experience, their daily
> walks of life, in such a manner, in such an under-
> standable way that the yoke becomes easy, the bur-
> dens become light. He has given that he that is
> faithful shall wear the crown of life; he that has been
> faithful even unto the end, he who has known and
> who does know all manners of temptations that
> come to the hearts, the minds, the souls of men,
> both mentally and materially . . . will make self a
> channel for the expressions of that love which *made*
> Him the Savior of men. 413-3

Our crosses should no longer be seen as sufferings or

even as hardships. Instead, each of the experiences we bear in life are our own individualized opportunity to have a part in the fulfillment of God's divine plan— *bringing all of humankind to an awareness of its relationship with the Creator.* Through service to others, and our own development, we become a part of this great work. Without overcoming those things which keep us out of harmony from a perfect attunement with God, we cannot hope to regain that Wholeness which was ours in the Beginning. Therefore, we must not attempt to shed or go around our own challenges and opportunities. There will come a time when we recognize the pattern of the Christ and follow in the footsteps of our Elder Brother:

> Hold fast to that ideal, and using Him ever as the Ideal. And hold up that *necessity* for each to meet the same problems. And *do not* attempt to shed . . . or go around the cross. *This* is that upon which each and every soul *must* look and know it is to be borne in self *with* Him. 5749-14

In other words, until we overcome our own crosses through the manifestation of the Christ Consciousness we cannot expect to attain the crown, which is the destiny of every soul:

> So, each in their respective lives, their own experiences, find their cross overcoming the world, overcoming those things, those conditions, those experiences, that would not only enable them to meet the issues of life but to become heirs with Him of the Crown of Glory. What, then, is this Crown of Glory? Does this bespeak only of those things, those conditions, that have to do with the spiritual life? Did the overcoming give the authority? Did the

overcoming make this Son of man the Lord, the
Glory, the Crown of Life? So He, as the pattern for
each, makes the way clear, the way open that each
soul—as it meets the crosses, endures the temptations and overcomes them—may become an heir,
joint heir with Him to the Crown of Glory; with
power temporal, power mental, power spiritual to
become the sons and daughters of God, as many as
are called—and all that fulfil that purpose for which
they, as individuals, are called—and carry on in that
manner, overcoming, meeting, bearing within
themselves. Not in sorrow, not in wailing, but in the
joy of the Lord. 262-36

CONCLUSION

Life is a purposeful experience. Ultimately, everything
that happens to us has the potential to remove all that
stands in the way of our perfect attunement with God.
Nothing comes our way that cannot be used as a means
of becoming a greater channel of God's love in the earth,
allowing His presence to fill every portion of our lives.
Nothing comes our way that cannot ultimately help us—
even if it is only that we might experience a challenge
first so that in time we might assist another with the
same problem. Life's opportunities can either weigh us
down, or we can use them as stepping stones toward
growth. In either case, we will come to learn obedience
and alignment to divine laws through the things that we
experience:

Life then is purposeful. What is life? It is a manifestation of a soul. Remember that self is body,
mind and soul. As the soul would know, does know,
it is the gift of the Creator, the Maker. The purpose
in life, then, is not the gratifying of appetites nor of

any selfish desires, but it is that the entity, the soul, may make the earth, where the entity finds its consciousness, a better place in which to live. 4047-2

Each entity enters a material experience for a purpose; not accidentally, not by chance. But life and its expressions are purposeful. And each experience is that the entity may become more and more a channel through which the knowledge and the application of Creative Forces may be made manifest in a material world. 1792-2

Regardless of where we find ourselves in life, regardless of what challenges we may have drawn to us in the present, through the activities of our attunement, service, and free will, our lives can be subject to His direction. By being grounded in a spiritual motivation, by relying upon the internal pattern of the Christ Consciousness, and by attempting to be a channel of God's love to others, our success is assured. Through service, we are helping our Elder Brother bring humankind to the fulfillment of its relationship with the Creator. Therefore, repeatedly, we are encouraged to begin each day with a prayer such as, "God, use me—my body, my mind, my soul—my whole being as a channel of blessing to someone today." But the choice is always ours to make: "This day there is set before thee life and death, good and evil—choose thou." Just as was demonstrated in the life of Jesus, only in bearing our crosses with a spiritual intent may we surmount any condition. As we place another's needs before our own, we open ourselves to becoming a more perfect channel of God's love in the earth. By becoming such a channel, the Creator's presence fills every aspect of our lives and our way becomes clear:

As He has given, and as has been presented again and again, not in times nor seasons, not in new moons nor in any place, but *every* day, *every* hour we show forth His love in a manner that makes for the knowledge of all contacting us that He walks with us, that He is our friend. 262-36 ,

Jesus showed mankind's destiny and ultimate potential. The first study group was told that this destiny was simply dependent upon their faithfulness.

LESSON ELEVEN

ONENESS

... for there is one God; and there is none other but he ...
Mark 12:32

MEDITATION AFFIRMATION

As my body, mind and soul are one, Thou, O Lord, in the manifestations in the earth, in power, in might, in glory, art one. May I see in that I do, day by day, more of that realization, and manifest the more. 262-38

ONENESS

Introduction

The first lesson for six months *should be* One—One—
One—One; *oneness of God, oneness of man's relation,
oneness of force, oneness of time, oneness of purpose,* oneness *in every effort—oneness—oneness!* 900-429

Where is *thine* own *will? One with* His, *or to the glorifying
of thine own desires—thine own selfish interests?*
262-42

One of the great ironies of human nature is the fact that
the very structure intended to enrich our relationship
with God is the one thing which divides us most as a human family. For countless eons, more wars have been
fought on religious principles than for any other reason.
Even to this day, wars, bloodshed, political battles, and
countless examples of our inhumanity to one another
are commonplace as one group tries to instill (or en-
force) their belief systems, their politics, or the su-
premacy of *their* God onto the lives of others.

These conflicts are not simply between various religions but are also within each denomination. There are
sects within Christianity, Buddhism, Judaism, Hindu-
ism, Islam—*within every religion!*—many convinced
that they are just a little more right than anyone else.
Even various churches, temples, and synagogues have
found differences with other members of their own sect
who have somehow fallen away from the "original" or
the "true" faith.

In addition to separating people from one another,
these conflicts have also caused individuals to become
disillusioned with religion—some even becoming con-

vinced that religion is a waste of time. Too often the result has been that people have given up their faith in God because of their disappointment in humankind.

Interestingly enough, the Edgar Cayce material states that part of the problem is due to our ignorance of our O*neness* with one another. Cayce's information presents a hopeful and inspiring approach to spirituality and religion that inextricably weaves all of humanity together. Rather than focusing upon the form of specific religions or dogmas, the readings instead focus upon the importance of every single soul attempting to manifest an awareness of the living Spirit in the earth. In fact, in response to a question regarding religious orthodoxy, Cayce stated:

> . . . what is the difference? . . . Truth . . . is of the one source. Are there not trees of oak, of ash, of pine? There are the needs of these for meeting this or that experience . . . Then, all will fill their place. Find not fault with *any*, but rather show forth as to just how good a pine, or ash, or oak, or *vine*, thou art! 254-87

From Cayce's perspective, our goal is not to simply wait for heaven; our goal is not to escape the earth, instead we are challenged to bring an awareness of the Creator into our lives and into our surroundings wherever we may be, right now.

There is a common bond we all share as a collective humanity: *there is but one God and we are all God's children.* In order to reawaken that sense of connectedness we share with one another, the readings state that the start of any spiritual journey should begin with the knowledge that *the Lord God is One.* Regardless of the name we call that God by, or the religions on earth which we feel drawn to, there is but One Creator, One Source,

One Law. In fact, perhaps more than anything else, this concept of "Oneness" is the underlying philosophy of the Edgar Cayce readings.

JUST WHAT IS ONENESS?

This notion of Oneness in a world so filled with variety may, at first, seem a difficult concept to comprehend. After all, we are surrounded by a myriad of plants, trees, animals, experiences, and people. Rather than attempting to make all things the same, however, Oneness suggests instead that we have the opportunity to view this rich diversity as an example of the multiple ways in which the *one Spirit* tries to find expression in our lives. Since there is only one God—the source of all that exists—ultimately, the universe must be composed of only One Force.

Oneness as a force implies that all things are interrelated. Every one of us has a connection to one another, the earth, the universe, and to God. This one force is a force for good which is attempting to bring the spirituality of the Creator into the earth. Unfortunately, because of our limited awareness of the power of free will, individuals are able to direct that force into selfish purposes and desires, creating "evil" in the process.

The good news is that in spite of how things may appear in the world today, the readings assert that all of Creation will eventually be brought into an awareness of this Oneness and of the Law of Love which it implies. One of our challenges as individuals is to make the world a better place because we have lived in it. Perhaps the best approach to this consciousness is reflected in the Bible when it states that we must love God with all our heart, mind, and soul, and our neighbor as ourselves.

In terms of spirituality, the concept of Oneness suggests that God is not limited to expressing through one religion alone. Instead, the Creator manifests in individuals' lives because of their faith and because of their relationship to the spiritual Source, not because of their specific religion. From Cayce's perspective, religion is the form in which individuals attempt to understand the manifestation of this Spirit. God can (and does!) work through every soul in the earth.

As a means of discovering the Oneness of spirit, the readings encourage comparative religious study. Through such a discipline each of us might see beyond surface differences and instead find the commonalties we share with one another:

> . . . *coordinate* the teachings, the philosophies of the East and the West, the Oriental and the Occidental, the new truths and the old . . . Correlate not the differences, but where all religions meet—*there is one God!* "Know, O Israel, the Lord thy God is *one!*"
> 991-1

When the concept of reincarnation is studied, what becomes apparent is not what religion people may be in the present, rather what is most important is how individuals apply the knowledge they possess. Within the cycle of reincarnation, we have all been Jewish, we have all been students of Eastern or Middle Eastern religions, we have all been agnostic or even atheistic, we have all been Christian. It's important to remember that, first, we are all children of the same God, and only secondly are we separated by doctrines or specific religious beliefs. We are spiritual beings manifesting in the physical world. Our religious dogmas and beliefs have changed as readily as we have. To be bigoted toward any situation, type of individual, or experience—especially with the knowledge that we will draw those same circumstances to us in the future—is not in keeping with the concept of Oneness.

In discussing religious denominations, the readings state:

> . . . consider a field of corn. In the grain of corn there is life. Man plants it in the soil, works it, and then he reaps the harvest. Not every man selects the same kind of corn. Not every man plows it alike. Not every man sows it alike. Not every man reaps it alike. Yet in each case it brings forth the very best that there is. It is the God or the life within each grain that the man is seeking. It sustains his body, and also produces seed to raise more. That's religion. That's the denominations. 294-161

RELIGION AS A FORM

The work of Edgar Cayce has attracted individuals from all walks of life and religious backgrounds. In fact, Cayce's view was that if the information in the readings was helpful and hopeful, making you a better person in the process, then you should be able to bring that renewed sense of "spirit" into your own faith. If, on the other hand, working with a particular concept wasn't helpful to you (the philosophy of reincarnation being one example), then individuals were simply told to leave it alone. Individuals were never advised to change their religious beliefs because of the Cayce readings. What Cayce was most concerned with was the *application* of spiritual principles not an individual's specific religion. There is a difference between spirituality and religion, *although both are important.*

Religion is primarily concerned with matters of religious faith, ritual, structure and tradition. Unfortunately, too often a specific religion has been seen as the vehicle for personal salvation rather than simply being one of the various forms in which humankind is trying to understand the manifestation of spirit in their lives. Many individuals have somehow elevated one religion above all others, perhaps deciding that there is but one form with which to demonstrate true faith. On the other hand, at times it has been the very religious structure with which individuals have become frustrated or disappointed, perhaps even deciding that they no longer need to have religion in their lives. Neither of these responses is in keeping with the concept of Oneness. It is important to remember that religion serves a purpose. Without some form, spirituality can too easily become simply a philosophical mind-game rather than having practical ramifications for daily life. Loose spirituality may be fragmented, selfishly independent, lacking community, etc. Without religious form, children can be raised without a sense of the applicability of spirit in their lives.

One of our confusions associated with religion is that we often mistake the form for the spirit. For example, individuals may have a particularly moving religious experience while attending a particular church or a specific religious denomination. These experiences may be such things as being overwhelmed by the spirit, having a very moving (or even a "kundalini") experience, awakening to the awareness of God's presence, even speaking in tongues. Rather than seeing these experiences within the context of form, however, individuals often assume that because their experience was valid, everything else associated with that religious form contains the same degree of value—they are only forgetting that throughout the history of humankind, individuals have had similar transformational experiences in *every* religion.

Regarding the various religious forms, the readings state:

There may be different channels of approach, yes. For not all peoples walked in the field when the wheat was ripe. Neither did all stand at the tomb when Lazarus was called forth. Neither were they all present when He walked on the water, nor when He fed the five thousand, nor when He hung on the cross. Yet each experience answered, and does answer to something within each individual soul-entity. For each soul is a corpuscle in the body of God. 3395-2

One of the readings states, " . . . God loveth those who love Him, whether they be called of this or that sect or schism or ism or cult! The Lord is *one!*" (3976-27) Remember, the essential premise of the Cayce philosophy is that we are all attempting to manifest the Christ Consciousness in the earth. Although we might currently find ourselves in the physical dimension, we are not physical creatures with souls, rather we are souls who happen to be expressing ourselves in materiality. The distinction is important because too often we may associate ourselves with external, temporal things such as race, sexuality, color, and religion that are not a part of our true spiritual nature. It is not so much that we *go* to heaven, rather we *grow* in awareness of our true spiritual nature and of our relationship with God and with one another. In fact, this process of growth and unfoldment is clearly described in the New Testament (Matthew 13:31-33 or Luke 13:81-21) when Jesus discusses the nature of heaven in parables:

Another parable put he forth unto them, saying, The kingdom of heaven is like to a grain of mustard seed, which a man took, and sowed in his field: which indeed is the least of all seeds: but when it is grown, it is the greatest among herbs, and becometh a tree, so that the birds of the air come and lodge in the branches thereof. Another parable spake he unto them; the kingdom of heaven is like unto leaven, which a woman took, and hid in three measure of meal, till the whole was leavened.

And, from the readings, "For you grow to heaven, you don't go to heaven. It is within thine own conscience that ye grow there." (3409-1)

SPIRITUALITY AS A LIVING AWARENESS

Although religion often deals with form, spirituality generally deals with an individual's application of his or her individual knowledge or awareness. Since our natural state is spirit, reawakening to full spiritual awareness is one of the purposes we all have in common. In fact, in one reading (3357-2), Cayce states that "Soul development should take precedence over all things." From the readings' perspective, this development is not achieved through some great deed or act, instead it is a gradual accomplishment which is attained "line upon line, precept upon precept." What appears to be most important in terms of soul development is an individual's application of the things of the spirit in their interactions with others: love, kindness, gentleness, patience, persistence, and consistency.

Since the purpose of life is to bring the spirituality of the Creator into the earth, attunement and application are at the heart of spiritual growth. Attunement is the process of reawakening to an awareness of our spiritual nature and our true relationship with God. As mentioned previously, the most frequently recommended tools for achieving this attunement are the regular practice of prayer and meditation. Both prayer and medita-

tion are invaluable at reestablishing a conscious awareness of our spiritual source while inviting God's will to
work through us as a "channel of His blessings" in service to others.

Repeatedly, a core concept from the Edgar Cayce
material has been stated: "Spirit is the life, mind is the
builder, and the physical is the result." In terms of Oneness, essentially what this means is that the one force,
spirit, constantly flows through us. However, it is acted
upon by the properties of the mind and then channeled
into everyone's life in accordance with their free will.
Regardless of whether or not an individual even believes
in God, everything about that person is given life
through the properties of the one activating spirit. What
he or she does with that spirit is a matter of choice and
"crimes or miracles" may be the result.

This ability of personal creation, whether through
thought, experience, or activity, caused the readings to
identify the human soul as a "co-creator with God." Because of this gift of co-creation, Cayce continually advised individuals that one of the most important things
they could do was to establish an appropriate spiritual
motivation (or ideal) for their lives, thereby directing
personal choice into positive directions. From Cayce's
perspective, too often we are out of touch with the intentionality (the *why*) behind our everyday actions. By
consciously establishing a spiritual motivation such as
service, or compassion, or love, or Jesus as our pattern,
and then trying to make that motivation a greater part of
our lives, real personal transformation and soul development can result.

Just like in the story of the Prodigal Son (Luke 15:11-
32), we were with God in the beginning and through
choice and experience found ourselves cut off from a
complete awareness of Him. In one respect, the "Fall of
Humankind" was really our descent in consciousness

from the realms of infinity to those of time and space. However, this was not necessarily a "bad thing" or an erroneous choice. Just as a child learns through experience, choice, and making mistakes along the way, our own experiences through choice and will embody a maturation process that will enable us to come into our full heritage and an awareness of our true spiritual nature. In time, as we bring the spirituality of God into the earth, we will awaken to our own spiritual *Source*, eventually finding our way back to the Creator.

> The soul, then, must return—*will* return—to its Maker. It is a portion of the Creative Forces, which is energized . . . even in materiality, in the flesh . . . Then, just being kind, just being patient, just showing love for thy fellow man; *that* is the manner in which an individual works *at* becoming aware of the consciousness of the Christ Spirit. 272-9

Not only is spiritual transformation our goal, but it is our birthright as well. With the proper spiritual motivation, we will be brought into alignment with this perfect pattern by working with *attunement*, appropriate mental *attitudes*, and a desire to bring our spiritual ideal into physical *application*.

JESUS REVISITED

Throughout history, the perspectives people have had on the life and teachings of Jesus have been varied, oftentimes even at odds. For some, Jesus has been seen as the only Son of God, bringing salvation only to those who called themselves Christian. Members of non-Christian religions may have ignored his life and ministry or they may have thought, "Christians have been cruel to me and therefore I'm not interested in Jesus."

Individuals involved in New Thought or comparable religions may have decided that Jesus was "just a teacher," or they may have disregarded him altogether. According to the Edgar Cayce readings, each of these perspectives is short-sighted.

Although Edgar Cayce was a Sunday school teacher all of his life, as well as an elder in the Presbyterian church, for him the meaning of Jesus' life went beyond that described by Christians and non-Christians alike. For that reason, regardless of our upbringing or our religious affiliation, the Cayce material offers some insightful and challenging information about the life and work of this man Jesus who became the Christ.

Essentially, the readings present Jesus as our "Elder Brother," a soul who came to show each one of us the way back to our spiritual Source by perfectly manifesting the laws of the Creator. Part of his mission was to fully demonstrate the living awareness of the spirit in the earth—something each one of us will eventually have to do. Therefore, Jesus' life of service to others serves as an example for all of humankind. In fact, the readings state:

> For the Master, Jesus, even the Christ, is the pattern for every man in the earth, whether he be Gentile or Jew, Parthenian or Greek. For all have the pattern, whether they call on that name or not . . . 3528-1

Jesus Himself states, "I am in my Father, and ye in me, and I in you." (John 14:20) We are all part of that same spiritual Source. Jesus was a child of God—just as we are all Children of God. What Jesus did, we are all being called to do, and, as our Elder Brother and Pattern He will show us the Way. In fact, Jesus is the Good Shepherd who is very much involved *right now* in pulling together God's flock, and teaching us about our relationship with the Creator. In discussing with God our joint spiritual nature and eventual destiny, Jesus states:

> They are not of the world, even as I am not of the world ... That they all may be one; as thou, Father, art in me, and I in thee, that they also may be one in us: that the world may believe that thou hast sent me. And the glory which thou gavest me I have given them; that they may be one, even as we are one: I in them, and thou in me, that they may be made perfect in one; and that the world may know that thou hast sent me, and hast loved them, as thou hast loved me.
>
> John 17:16, 21-23

The importance of this information—the fact that every individual is an integral part of God's flock and that *we all share the same relationship with the Creator as even Jesus*—will eventually transform (even *revolutionize!*) the ways in which we think about ourselves and treat one another.

CONCLUSION

Why do we have so many religious sects if the principle of Oneness is an undergirding force in the universe? In part, the answer lies in our own diversity and in the fact that we are all drawn to what we need at a given time for our own personal growth and development. In addition, we also possess the very human trait of wanting to "pin down" our truth, putting parameters around our understanding so that we can deal with it. But truth is a growing thing and the Cayce readings affirm that no one has all the answers to the marvelous question of who we really are as God's spiritual children. But even in the midst of our diversity, we share a common spiritual heri-

tage. We are all Children of the same God. We are all part
of the one spiritual Source, our Creator, our Mother/Fa-
ther, our God:

> Each soul in entering the material experience
> does so for those purposes of advancement towards
> that awareness of being fully conscious of the one-
> ness with the Creative Forces. 2632-1

Oneness as a force suggests that each of us is con-
nected in ways that we might never have before imagined. Our challenge is to bring that Wholeness to
consciousness, an "awareness within each soul, imprinted in pattern on the mind and waiting to be awakened by the will, of the soul's oneness with God."
(5749-14) Regardless of an individual's religion or personal beliefs, this Christ pattern exists in potential upon
the very fiber of their being. It is that part of us which is
in perfect accord with the Creator and is simply waiting
to find manifestation in our lives:

> For indeed in Him, the Father-God, ye move and
> have thy being. Act like it! Don't act like ye think ye
> are a god! Ye may become such, but when ye do ye
> think not of thyself. For what is the pattern? He
> thought it not robbery to make Himself equal with
> God, but He acted like it in the earth. He made Him-
> self of no estate that you, through His grace, through
> His mercy, through His sacrifice might have an ad-
> vocate with that First Cause, God; that first prin-
> ciple, spirit. 4083-1

LOVE

And now faith, hope, and love abide. These three; and the greatest of these is love.   I Corinthians 13:13 (NRSV)

MEDITATION AFFIRMATION

Our Father, through the love that Thou hast manifested in the world through Thy Son, the Christ, make us more aware of "God is love." 262-43

LOVE

Introduction

"Thou shalt love the Lord thy God with all thy heart, thy mind, thy soul; thy neighbor as thyself." For this is the whole *law—the* whole *law.* 262-100

. . . the culmination of this series of lessons will be love; *for He so loved the world as to give His Son, His Self, that man should come to the realization of the oneness of the Father in the earth.* 262-38

Oftentimes, when we hear the word 'love' it conjures up images of romance or passion. Or, perhaps, we think of love as being descriptive of a relationship we share with another individual—a parent, a companion, a friend, or a child. And although these are certainly indications of love, they do not adequately describe the nature of love itself. Love is much more than a human emotion. True love reaches out to others without regard as to what is received in return. Ultimately, it is a state of being that enables God to continually work through us as a channel of His blessings.

From the perspective of the Edgar Cayce readings, the entire purpose of life is to let the love of God manifest through us into the earth. Therefore, love can be the greatest service we can offer another. In fact, in a very real sense, love is the basis for all we should be about:

The children of light first love, for "Though I may have the gift of prophecy, though I may speak in unknown tongues, though I give my body to be burned and have not the spirit of the Son of man, the Christ Consciousness, the Christ Spirit, I am nothing." For, the children of light *know* Him; He calleth each by name. 262-46

Despite the demands of material life, only love really matters. Only by our willingness to express unconditional love will the Creative Forces be able to work in and through us. Love is the perfect fruit of the spirit. It is giving out the very best that we have—the very best that we know. It is a powerful expression of healing. It is a great teacher. It allows for the realization of one's purpose in life, for only through love may spirit become manifested in the earth.

Unconditional love—divine love—is universal. For that reason, true love knows no preference. According to Cayce, there is a strong correlation between the concept of Oneness and this lesson of love. In simplest terms, oneness relates to the universality of the *One Force* and divine love can be regarded as the expression of that force. In an effort to describe the ways in which the universality of God's love could be expressed, Edgar Cayce told members of the first study group that they were not limited in how they might personally experience the Creator's love:

Each may find in this that which is being sought . . . in that expressed in a baby's smile; in the hope, the light, the seeking, the manifestation of that which is love undefiled. The next may see it in the rose, as it seeks—with that it has to do with—to make manifest that beauty in expression that may *glorify* its Maker. The next may find it in friendship, in that which speaks without thought of self, that which makes for the expressions of love *glorified* through the friendliness that comes with friendship. The next may find it in that as reasons for the beauty of a song, in the harmony that shows forth in the expression of the soul within; whether in instruments or the soul raised in praise to the Giver of light. The next may find it in the expressions of the duty that may be the lot of one that, without thought of self, shows forth in the acts of life that first thought of the duty from a material standpoint, yet the *love* made manifest from wholly showing forth His life, His love, till He come again! The next may find it in the manner of speech under the varied circumstances that arise in the experience of all, through that association which comes in the daily walks of life, and in the encouragement that may be given through the kind word spoken; the giving of the cup of water to anyone seeking, to those that thirst. This may show to such an one the love that is manifest in "God is love." The next may find it in whatever the hands find to do, that done well, in all phases of one's experience, that lends self in the daily walks of life, doing the best with that which presents itself, in the glorying of the expressions, "As ye do it unto the least of these, my little ones, ye do it unto me." The next will find it in the glory that comes in the satisfaction of a contented heart, in knowing that each day has brought an opportunity that has been taken advantage of by self in showing the kindness here, going out of the way in self's own life to make the lot of a neighbor more joyous, brighter, in the activities of the daily life. The next may find it in looking forward to those days that may come, for the filling of those places that may be made or given in the lives spent in the service of Him who may call that thy face be that which may bring the knowledge of thine life, thine heart, spent in His service day by day. 262-45

In other words, love is a state of being that can be

found whenever we abide in His Consciousness. Whenever we seek to become a channel of His Blessings, fulfilling that which we were born to do—love is expressed. Love is the condition that sparks our inner wholeness into manifestation. In time, as our awareness expands, we will discover that love is of God and, just like our Creator, it is everywhere.

THE GREAT COMMANDMENT

In discussing the importance of love, the Cayce readings repeatedly referred individuals to the "Great Commandment." Found in the New Testament, the information was given by our Elder brother in response to a question regarding the greatest law set down by Moses:

> Thou shalt love the Lord thy God with all thy heart, and with all thy soul, and with all thy mind. This is the first and great commandment. And the second is like unto it, Thou shalt love thy neighbor as thyself.
>
> Matthew 22:37-39

Echoing that same focus, the Cayce material states:

> The first and the last commandments are the whole law: *Thou shalt love the Lord thy God with all thy heart, thy mind, thy soul, thy body; and thy neighbor as thyself.* The rest only explains, only interprets, only manifests for the individual the tenets of the law. For the law is love, and love is law. And the Lord is one in same. 2905-3

Immediately we are struck by the information that we are to love God first. We might say, "Okay, that makes sense" or, on the other hand, we may even wonder why?

Why does the Great Commandment ask us to love God first? In one respect, perhaps if we can truly learn to love God, then everything else will somehow fall into place. During those moments when we are truly manifesting a love for God, we have the opportunity to see every human being as an expression of the Creator's love. According to the readings, when love is truly a portion of our awareness, it may be experienced in a baby's smile, in the beauty of a rose as it unfolds, in a friendship that gives no thought of self—in fact, love can be found everywhere.

Another way of looking at the readings emphasis on the Great Commandment ties into our purpose for being in the earth in the first place: *to somehow become a channel of blessings—a channel of God's love—unto others*. In the language of the readings:

Keep the heart singing. Look not upon the service to Him as being *duty;* rather as the privilege to show forth in thine life, thine experience, the blessings that have been and that may be thine in an *opportunity* of service to thy fellow man. In this manner, in this way, may the greater joys, the greater blessings, come into thine own experience. And know ye that unless the experience is thine own to thine own soul, it is only theory. Yet, as ye live day by day in the opportunities of the service of being a channel of blessing, so may thine own life, thine own experience in the present, be enriched in the Lord. 473-1

Members of the first study group were told what type of personal awareness was the ultimate goal:

When ye love God better than yourself! Then is it the day, the hour, of the awakening in thine self! to do His service, to do His biddings, to be—as it were—a *sacrifice* in all those things that make for *burnings,* for *longings* for those things that make for the weakening of the flesh; that ye may know that He will have His way with thee. Becoming selfless, becoming conscious of His Spirit, His love, moving in and through thee, prompting thee in thy words, thy activities, thy service. 262-59

In other words, the Great Commandment is about love in its highest form. It isn't merely affection or passion, it isn't possessive or conditional, it is never jealous or insecure. The Great Commandment is about cultivating love as a state of our own awareness: giving out the very best within us, with no thought of receiving in return.

LOVE IS GIVING

Sometimes, that which we have come to call "love" can be selfish. Selfish love is a love that feels limited in supply, therefore our desire is to reach out and pull it toward ourselves. Conversely, selfless love is without bounds or limits. Rather than a love which we pull toward ourselves, selfless love is one which flows through us to others. Our capacity to share this love grows as we grow. In fact, the entire process of life is one of personal growth and transformation. But the growth comes only as our pattern of wholeness unfolds in our interaction and selfless service and love toward others. Essentially, this unfoldment is the process which enables us to truly love one another—just as we are loved by the Creator. It is a growth whereby we recognize the Law of Love—a law perhaps best expressed as "giving in action":

Q. *What is the law of love?*
A. Giving. As is given in this injunction, "Love thy

neighbor as thyself." As is given in the injunction, "Love the Lord thy God with all thine heart, thine soul and thine body" . . . Remember there is no greater than the injunction, "God so loved His creation, or the world, as to give His only begotten Son, for their redemption." Through that love, as man makes it manifest in his own heart and life, does it reach that law, and in compliance of a law, the law becomes a part of the individual. *That is the law of love.* Giving in action, without the force felt, expressed, manifested, shown, desired or reward for that given . . . So we have *love* is *law, law is love. God is love. Love is God.* 3744-5

Repeatedly the readings state that God so loved the world that He gave all that He possessed to His Creation: *the ability to become at-one with Him.* Just as love is giving forth the very best within us, ultimately selfless acts of creation are brought about in the very same manner. In fact, one reading (262-46) states that all of Creation was brought into manifestation through love.

For each blade of grass, each blossom, each tree, each crag, each mountain, each river, each lake is as a gift from the Creative Forces in man's experience that he may know more of the love of God. And as a soul, as a developing body then sees in the creatures, in the various kingdoms as *they* care for their young, as they are selective in their mating, as they are mindful of the influences and the environs, learn from these Nature's lessons or God's expression to the children of men; that He indeed is in His holy temple and is *mindful* of man's estate—if *man* minds the *laws* of nature, of God. For love is law, love is God. 1248-1

The power and all-pervading aspects of such love surpasses our understanding. But just as Jesus came to realize this relationship, manifesting the love of God in the earth, we too are called to such a service. As children of God we can express that sense of divine love as we allow our Creator to have His way in our lives. Continually, we are challenged to bring to conscious awareness the significance of our heritage and our relationship with the Creative Forces:

> Have ye looked into thy heart lately? What manner of image cherisheth thou there? Does it take hold upon the earth, or those things that are earthy? or does it take hold upon those celestial things of beauty and hope—no hate, no jealousy, no *desire* to laud self or others, but only to know Him who hath given, "If ye love me, keep my commandments; and my commandments are not grievous—my yoke is easy, my burden is light," to those who *love* His coming. Hast thou entertained thy Lord, thy God, lately? *Why* not? Hast thou been kind and loving, and patient, to any today? *Why* not? Hast thou been showing the outward appearances; that ye may be well-spoken of or thought of? *Why?* Study to show thyself approved unto *God*—not to man! a workman *not* ashamed; keeping self from ever *condemning* others! Condemn not, if ye would not be condemned. This is law—*divine* law! Do ye seek to know divine law? Ye can only find it in thyself. 294-198

As we strive to fulfill less and less of our own selfish desires, and instead place another's needs before our own—becoming a true channel of blessings—more and more do the qualities of the spirit become a portion of our conscious lives. As we live in a manner that allows for this expression of Wholeness in the earth, we gain an awareness of the soul and its longing to be used by the

Creative Forces. True love asks nothing in return. It flows
forth in abundant supply for the sake of love itself.

THE MANIFESTATION OF LOVE

How, then, may the entity—with the knowledge
of its own self's activities in the earth, through its
varied experiences in same—go about to apply
same, to become more and more aware of its at-
oneness, its consciousness *of* its at-oneness with
that consciousness of *being* one with this applied
law, this applied love in its experience? As has been
given, "Do that thou *knowest* to *do today,* and *then*
the next step may be given thee" . . . And ye come
more and more, by such living, to the awareness of
His presence abiding with thee! Not unto vainglorying, not unto self-consciousness; but rather
that "Here am I, Lord, use me. Let *me* be that channel of blessing to *someone today;* that Thy love, Thy
glory, Thy oneness, may be the greater manifested
in not only my experience but those that I contact
day by day." 601-11

Since the Great Commandment reminds us of the importance of loving God with our whole heart, mind, and
soul, we might ask how we can apply this in our everyday lives? Simply put, it is through prayer, meditation,
and application. In fact, ultimately prayer and meditation are instrumental in assisting us in learning how to
love. In addition, it is in meditation that we can experience the true love of the Divine. The reason is because
through attunement, the divine pattern within is quickened to become a greater portion of conscious awareness.
And essentially, the pattern of the Christ Consciousness
is one of love:

Let that mind be in thee which was in Christ. Not

of self, but that others may know the love of God. So live, then, as to manifest that love. 281-65

Since God is love, love's supply is everlasting. When we have a friend or a loved one, the love we possess for that individual is not lessened as we make other friendships. The way we unconditionally love the one individual we hold most dear in our hearts is the same manner we must come to feel about every person who comes into our lives. Ultimately, we must learn to love even our worst "enemies," even those who don't appear to love us in return:

For he that cherisheth the love that is without dissimulation, that is without favor, that is without those things of self-indulgence or self-aggrandizement, maketh for that way that may be opened to self for the greater and greater understanding. 470-11

In the Scriptures, Jesus emphasized the importance of our love for others. In fact, He gave a "new commandment" (John 13:34) which states: "That you love one another; as I have loved you." According to Edgar Cayce, that love was one of complete selflessness. When we are truly able to love another person in selflessness, then that person's relationship with his or herself as well as that person's relationship with God becomes more important than the individual's relationship with us. It is a love in which there is no thought of personal gain. A simple example might be expressed in attentive listening. Just try to find the time to listen fully to another person—not trying to provide any answers, just attempt to be truly present as a listening ear to someone in need. Just as being quiet in ourselves allows us to better hear another person, so does setting aside our personal motives allows us to be a better channel of love to others.

For many of us, one of the most difficult lessons we face is to learn to love ourselves. Even though the love of others is crucial to a love-filled life, it is possible only when balanced by a love of self. In fact, whenever individuals wanted to know how they could improve specific relationships—learning how to better love someone else—the readings advised them that an important step (in addition to being of service and doing what the individual knew to do) was to better love and understand themselves. At times, this may appear difficult. And yet, we must strive to remember that within, each of us has the potential to be whole and to be a channel of divine love.

Self in the physical grows weary, because you are only human, because you are finite; you have a beginning, you have an end of your patience, your love, your hope, your fear, your desire. These are to be considered also; not as unto self, but when these problems arise know, as He has given, you cannot walk the whole way alone, but He has promised in the Christ Consciousness to give you strength, to give you life and that more abundant. 3161-1

In order to grow toward the heritage of our destiny, we must begin to love ourselves (and one another) in the same manner that we are loved by God.

For as each individual realizes, as these tenets may be analyzed, if God had condemned—what opportunity would there be for man to find his way back to God? Thus each individual must do unto others as he would have his Brother, the Christ, his God, the Father, do unto him; and indeed, then, apply first, last and always His "Forgive, O God, as I forgive others. Find fault in me, O God, as I find fault in my brother." Less and less then of self, more and more of perfect love, without dissimulations, keeping that faith. Know that as there is the activity of self, self can only sow the seed of truth. And it will be to each individual as was indicated to the children of Israel. They entered into the Promised Land not because of their righteousness but because of the love of the Father for those who tried, who *tried* to live the righteousness. 5758-1

CONCLUSION

For, these are times and occasions when every effort should be made to preserve the universality of *love* as was and is presented by those who seek the way through *Him*—who is the light of the world! 877-29

God's love is boundless. Just as the sun sends forth its warmth and light upon everyone and everything without judgment or conditions, the love of God falls upon everyone equally. The Creator loves the just and the unjust, the good and the bad, those who possess faith and those who have lost it, those we hate as well as those we love, unconditionally. God's love is available in every circumstance, in every activity—its presence is woven throughout all of Creation. To love the Lord our God with all our hearts, our minds, our bodies and to love our neighbor as ourselves is the whole of God's law—it is our purpose for being in the earth:

For this purpose ye came into this experience; that ye might *glorify* that consciousness, that awareness of His presence, of His Spirit abiding with thee. Ye give manifestations of same in the manner, in the way in which ye measure that love to others about thee day by day. 1348-1

For, remember the law. It is the little leaven that leaveneth the whole lump. Again would it be repeated—it is here a little, there a little, line upon line, precept upon precept. Not that man does not know, has not heard of those activities necessary in each individual life to bring the joyous day of the Lord, but he needs to be reminded again and again. For, all are children and are seeking their way; oft groping blindly, following those that would lead here or there, when there needs to be the reminding that we must love one another—even as God has loved man and has made manifest that love . . . if those that seek will but open their hearts, their eyes, their minds to the wondrous love which God, the Father, has bestowed upon the children of men. 254-110

Love is not a thing to behold, rather it is an awareness to be lived. Divine love is love in its highest form. It is a state of consciousness that allows the Divine to work through us. It isn't possessive or conditional. It is never jealous or insecure. It is undergirded by a consciousness of oneness, because the imprint of the Creator is upon everything in the universe.

Regardless of who or where we are, ultimately, it is our heritage to fulfill that for which we were created. We have the ability to set ourselves aside and choose to be a channel of God's activity in the earth. Only in this manner do we cooperate fully with the Creative Forces. We have forgotten our relationship with the Divine. We are children of God with the responsibility of bringing His spirit into the earth. If we would truly come to know ourselves as we are known by God, it will require attunement and application.

One of the most important things we can do is to choose an appropriate motivation and ideal for our lives and allow the mind of Christ to manifest in us. As we choose right thought and right action, we cultivate a faith deep within us. As our faith grows, so too does our capacity to be used as a channel of spirit. Our life becomes more virtuous and our understanding expands as an expression of our inner wholeness.

All soul's share this same pattern of Wholeness which ever seeks to find expression. With fellowship we gain the realization of this connection with one another and our joint connection to God. And in patience we will be in greater possession of the soul's ability to allow God's love, laws, and presence to flow through our lives into manifestation.

Regardless of where we find ourselves right now, the Christ Consciousness stands at the doorway of our present consciousness. This Christ Pattern will enable us to come to the realization that we always abide in His presence. All we must do to express the Christ Spirit is to overcome those crosses that stand between us and our knowledge of that awareness—and He will assist us every step of the way. Since God is in all that exists, then all that exists is God. Through selflessness we can cultivate the awareness of that oneness and begin to live it. Ultimately, this awareness and its expression is God's greatest gift of love:

> To him, to her that is faithful, there shall be given a *crown* of light. And His name shall be above every name; for ye that have seen the light know in whom thou hast believed, and know that in thine own body, thine own mind, there is set the temple of the living God, and that it may function in thy dealings with thy fellow man in such measures that ye become as rivers of light, as fountains of knowledge,

as mountains of strength, as the pastures for the hungry, as the rest for the weary, as the strength for the weak. Keep the faith. 281-28

We are companions and co-creators with God. From this time on, let us manifest the love the Creator has for us—allowing that love to flow forth into all the earth. And, day by day, as we find ourselves doing that He would have us do, becoming channels of His blessings unto others, we will, at last, be worthy to be called Children of God.

Love is patient and kind; love is not jealous or boastful; it is not arrogant or rude. Love does not insist on its own way; it is not irritable or resentful; it does not rejoice at wrong, but rejoices in the right. Love bears all things, believes all things, hopes all things, endures all things . . . So faith, hope, love abide, these things; but the greatest of these is love. I Corinthians 13: 4-7, 13

MEDITATION AFFIRMATIONS

COOPERATION

Not my will but Thine, O Lord, be done in me and through me. Let me ever be a channel of blessings, today, now, to those that I contact, in every way. Let my going in, my coming out be in accord with that Thou would have me do, and as the call comes, "Here am I, send me, use me!"
Edgar Cayce reading 262-3

KNOW THYSELF

Father, as we seek to see and know Thy face, may we each, as individuals, and as a group, come to know ourselves, even as we are known, that we—as lights in Thee—may give the better concept of Thy Spirit in this world.
Edgar Cayce reading 262-5

IDEALS

God, be merciful to me! Help Thou my unbelief! Let me see in Him that Thou would have me see in my fellow man. Let me see in my brother that I see in Him whom I worship!
Edgar Cayce reading 262-11

FAITH

Create in me a pure heart, O God! Open Thou mine heart to the faith Thou hast implanted in all that seek Thy face! Help Thou mine unbelief in my God, in my neighbor, in myself!
Edgar Cayce reading 262-13

VIRTUE AND UNDERSTANDING

Let virtue and understanding be in me, for my defense is in Thee, O Lord, my Redeemer; for Thou hearest the prayer of the upright in heart.
Edgar Cayce reading 262-17

FELLOWSHIP

How excellent is Thy name in the earth, O Lord! Would I have fellowship with Thee, I must show brotherly love to my fellow man. Though I come in humbleness and have aught against my brother, my prayer, my meditation, does not rise to Thee. Help Thou my efforts in my approach to Thee.
Edgar Cayce reading 262-21

PATIENCE

How gracious is Thy presence in the earth, O Lord! Be Thou the guide, that we with patience may run the race which is set before us, looking to Thee, the Author, the Giver of light.
Edgar Cayce reading 262-24

THE OPEN DOOR
As the Father knoweth me, so may I know the Father, through the Christ Spirit, the door to the kingdom of the Father. Show Thou me the way.
Edgar Cayce reading 262-27

IN HIS PRESENCE
Our Father who art in heaven, may Thy kingdom come in earth through Thy presence in me, that the light of Thy word may shine unto those that I meet day by day. May Thy presence in my brother be such that I may glorify Thee. May I so conduct my own life that others may know Thy presence abides with me, and thus glorify Thee.
Edgar Cayce reading 262-30

THE CROSS AND THE CROWN
Our Father, our God, as we approach that that may give us a better insight of what He bore in the cross, what His glory may be in the crown, may Thy blessings—as promised through Him—be with us as we study together in His name.
Edgar Cayce reading 262-34

ONENESS
As my body, mind and soul are one, Thou, O Lord, in the manifestations in the earth, in power, in might, in glory, art one. May I see in that I do, day by day, more of that realization, and manifest the more
Edgar Cayce reading 262-38

LOVE
Our Father, through the love that Thou hast manifested in the world through Thy Son, the Christ, make us more aware of "God is love."
Edgar Cayce reading 262-43

For this commandment which I command thee this day, it is not hidden from thee, neither is it far off. It is not in heaven, that thou shouldest say, Who shall go up for us to heaven, and bring it unto us, that we may hear it, and do it? Neither is it beyond the sea, that thou shouldest say, Who shall go over the sea for us, and bring it unto us, that we may hear it, and do it? But the word is very nigh unto thee, in thy mouth, and in thy heart, that thou mayest do it.   Deuteronomy 30:11-14

Q. Should the Christ Consciousness be described as the awareness within each soul, imprinted in pattern on the mind and waiting to be awakened by the will, of the soul's oneness with God?
A. Correct. That's the idea exactly!
                                             Edgar Cayce reading 5749-14

. . . Thou shalt love the Lord thy God with all thy heart, and with all thy soul, and with all thy mind. This is the first and great commandment. And the second is like unto it, Thou shalt love thy neighbor as thyself.
                                             Matthew 22:37-39

The whole *law is to love the Lord thy God with all thy heart, thy mind, thy body; thy neighbor as thyself. This is the whole law, this is the whole purpose for an experience, an activity of an entity in any given or individual experience or appearance even throughout the sojourns in a material plane.*   Edgar Cayce reading 1464-2

Another parable put he forth unto them, saying, The kingdom of heaven is like to a grain of mustard seed, which a man took, and sowed in his field: Which indeed is the least of all seeds: but when it is grown, it is the greatest among herbs, and becometh a tree, so that the birds of the air come and lodge in the branches thereof. Another parable spake he unto them; The kingdom of heaven is like unto leaven, which a woman took, and hid in three measure of meal, till the whole was leavened.
                                             Matthew 13:31-33

For you grow to heaven, you don't go to heaven. It is within thine own conscience that ye grow there.
                                             Edgar Cayce reading 3409-1

A.R.E. PRESS

The A.R.E. Press publishes quality books, videos, and audiotapes meant to improve the quality of our readers' lives—personally, professionally, and spiritually. We hope our products support your endeavors to realize your career potential, to enhance your relationships, to improve your health, and to encourage you to make the changes necessary to live a loving, joyful, and fulfilling life.

Some titles related to *Twelve Lessons in Personal Spirituality,* along with their "stock numbers" in case you would like to order any of them directly from us, include:

A Search for God, Books I and II
In 1931, Edgar Cayce agreed to help a group of people grow spiritually and become more psychic. But there was one condition. They would have to *live* the precepts. It took the group eleven years to "live" the twenty-four chapters which became *A Search for God,* Books I and II, and thousands of people continue to study the principles today.
Book I only: ISBN 0-87604-000-8, 134 pp. Hardcover, **$9.95 #279**
Book II only: ISBN 0-87604-001-6, 133 pp. Hardcover, **$9.95 #280**

Experiments in a Search for God, by Mark Thurston, Ph.D.
Based on concepts from *A Search for God, Book I,* this valuable text will help you apply and live the universal concepts from the Edgar Cayce readings. For individual or group use. ISBN 0-87604-090-3, 139 pp. Paperback, **$10.95 #285**

Experiments in Practical Spirituality, by Mark Thurston, Ph.D.
Approximately 100 separate experiments help you apply universal laws in daily life. Based on the premise from the Edgar Cayce readings that we must live and apply something before we know it, this valuable book will help you grow to a more spiritual life. Keyed to *A Search for God, Book II.* ISBN 0-87604-122-5, 147 pp. Paperback, **$10.95 #304**

Your Life: Why It Is the Way It Is and What You Can Do About It/Understanding the Universal Laws, by Bruce McArthur

Bruce McArthur weaves a powerful narrative packed with how-to information which will help you create positive change in your life. Understanding and applying the universal laws will help you build financial security, attract loving relationships, solve difficult problems, and find your soul's true purpose. ISBN 0-87604-300-7, 276 pp. Paperback, **$14.95 #375**

The Edgar Cayce Ideals Workbook, by Kevin Todeschi

An earlier book by the author of *Twelve Lessons in Personal Spirituality,* this book will help you look at your ideals from many different angles, and its workbook format will guide you in harnessing their powerful motivating force for your life. ISBN 0-87604-259-0, 98 pp. Paperback, **$9.95 #350**

To order any of these books, or to receive a free catalog, call us at:

1-800-723-1112

Or write:

A.R.E. Press
215 67th Street
Virginia Beach, VA 23451-2061

A.R.E. PRESS

The A.R.E. Press publishes quality books, videos, and audiotapes meant to improve the quality of our readers' lives—personally, professionally, and spiritually. We hope our products support your endeavors to realize your career potential, to enhance your relationships, to improve your health, and to encourage you to make the changes necessary to live a loving, joyful, and fulfilling life.

For more information or to receive a free catalog, call:

1-800-723-1112

Or write:

A.R.E. Press
215 67th Street
Virginia Beach, VA 23451-2061

DISCOVER HOW THE EDGAR CAYCE MATERIAL CAN HELP YOU!

The Association for Research and Enlightenment, Inc. (A.R.E.®), was founded in 1931 by Edgar Cayce. Its international headquarters are in Virginia Beach, Virginia, where thousands of visitors come year round. Many more are helped and inspired by A.R.E.'s local activities in their own hometowns or by contact via mail (and now the Internet!) with A.R.E. headquarters.

People from all walks of life, all around the world, have discovered meaningful and life-transforming insights in the A.R.E. programs and materials, which focus on such areas as personal spirituality, holistic health, dreams, family life, finding your best vocation, reincarnation, ESP, meditation, and soul growth in small-group settings. Call us today on our toll-free number:

1-800-333-4499

or

Explore our electronic visitors center on the
Internet: **http://www.edgarcayce.org.**

We'll be happy to tell you more about how the work of the A.R.E. can help you!

A.R.E.
215 67th Street
Virginia Beach, VA 23451-2061